bill goldsmith

# Food alla Florentine

# FOOD
## alla Florentine

NAOMI BARRY & BEPPE BELLINI

ILLUSTRATIONS BY BILL GOLDSMITH

1972

DOUBLEDAY & COMPANY, INC., GARDEN CITY, NEW YORK

*Table of Contents*

Introduction

## Naomi Barry

I was seduced into collaborating on this cookbook for the most selfish of reasons. I wanted Beppe's recipes for myself and it seemed the most expeditious way of getting them.

Giuseppe "Beppe" Bellini deals in Raphael and Della Robbia. He is organizer and dynamo of the great international Antiques Fair that takes place every other October in the Palazzo Strozzi. Here he has the scope to marry art and gastronomy in the truly grand Florentine manner. He once stunned visitors to the Fair by inviting five hundred of them to an authentic Renaissance banquet.

When Bellini travels, he comes back not only with rare pieces of art but with his luggage crammed with spices from India or kitchen gadgets from New York for the pleasure of his connoisseur friends. When he gives a dinner party in Florence either at his town house on the Arno or at his villa, Marignolle, the cook is often called to the dining room for a round of applause from the appreciative guests.

Beppe once gave me an insider's gourmet tour of his favorite city. As we strolled from one restaurant to another, he greeted a man carrying a shabby suitcase.

"He is my truffle supplier," Bellini explained nonchalantly, as if such a specialist were normal in everybody's daily routine.

The fellow opened the little suitcase, balanced it on his knee, and displayed his freshly gathered harvest of pungent white truffles. Bellini sniffed happily and ordered the whole lot to be delivered to his house, where they were to be used in green salads, in spaghetti sauce, or sprinkled over scallops of veal.

Friends wrote me not long ago, "We think one of Beppe's greatest character traits is how he approaches a restaurant. It is a great experience to follow him into a fine restaurant or a *trattoria*, right past the headwaiters and into the kitchen and see him inspect each pot on the cooking range. Very often a finger goes into the pot to gather a sample. Then he walks out with the chef beaming with pride at his attention.

"Also if Beppe thought a sauce needed a dash more of this or that he would talk it over with the chef and generally the chef would agree and affectionately embrace his, by then, best friend. And that's how Beppe ends up with so many good recipes."

## Giuseppe Bellini

I like working with my friends.

Sometimes I am surprised at my own persuasion, that I am able to convince my friends to work with me.

What often starts out as a laughing joke or a fantasy around the dining-room table frequently ends in a project that keeps us busy day and night until exhaustion. When this happens, I am even more amazed that we still remain friends.

The overwhelming success of the Florence International Antiques Fair is basically the achievement of my many friends who were willing to help me.

This cookbook is my friendship with Naomi Barry. It is easier for me to stir a sauce with a spoon than to make a *pasta fagioli* with words, but Naomi knows to take a stew and present it with clarity.

We first got together eating. She came to Florence to prepare a story on the gastronomy of the city for the American magazine *Gourmet*. We went to every restaurant in town, often hitting three during a single lunch.

Naomi Barry is well-known for her articles in the International *Herald Tribune*, for her monthly articles in *Gourmet*, for her book *Paris Personal*.

She travels constantly, led by her own lively curiosity. *Newsweek* once said of her and her newspaper column, "The indomitably high-spirited Naomi Barry has ranged the world to fill it. She has hawked apples in *les Halles de Paris*, hitchhiked to Italy to collect material, and once set out for Brussels by inland canal barge."

Naomi has the quality of direct simplicity. Her rule, "It has to be easy enough for me to do it. If you can explain it better, maybe it will be."

The composition of this book is due to her. Whenever I was vague (I was shocked to discover how often), she forced me to be logical and practical.

Frequently, I have been asked how to prepare this and that.

For the first time, however, someone has been able to pry my recipes from my fingertips and put them down on paper in such a way that they can be followed by anyone.

Don't think that this has not been a service, especially for me. From now on, I only have to consult the cookbook Naomi and I did together.

In 1959, my brother Mario and I started the Florence International Antiques Fair. The idea first came to us from our father who believed that such an international reunion would once again illuminate Florence in the eyes of the world as a great art market.

But parallel to the Antiques Fair, we seem to have established a gastronomic fair as well. It was a natural development.

As art dealers, we are people of the senses, receptive to architecture, painting, sculpture, tapestries, carpets, and the countless expressions of the minor arts.

We decided to make of our Antiques Fair a festival in honor of the senses. Sight, sound, odor, palate.

We set our tables with all the artistry we could summon up. We researched our dishes so that the foods were chosen with the same care that a painter selects and mixes the colors of his palette. To delight our ears, we had minstrels singing and playing in the background.

The guests supplied the rest. The brilliant and varied conversations. The clothes, the jewels, the careful grooming. Come to one of these bedazzling assemblies, and you will discover that banqueting is an Art, in the full sense of the word.

It is a strange analogy but the apex of any era in music seems to coincide with the periods of great advance in cooking. So the Renaissance kitchen triumphed to the sweetly melodic sounds of the viola da gamba and the lute. Later, little by little, the refined cuisines of the eighteenth-century courts of Italy and France were a fitting counterpoint to the music of Vivaldi, Mozart, Scarlatti. The mathematical serenity of Bach accompanies the quietly logical "Physiology of Taste" of Brillat-Savarin. The elaborate fantasy of the menus of Carême reflects the sublime romanticism of his contemporary, Beethoven.

The great dinners of the Fair have become already part of recent history, successors to the sumptuous banquets of the Medicis which caused wonderment and envy in all the courts of Europe.

More than tradition, however, prompted me to create this festive side of the Antiques Fair. I had personal reasons as well.

Among my earliest and happiest childhood memories were the joyous gatherings at my grandfather's country house in Impruneta at the time of the grape harvests. All of his friends and family would come to help the peasants pick the grapes.

When the work was done, big tables were set up on the threshing terrace. From six o'clock until midnight, the whole crowd together sat down in an atmosphere of gay friendship to eat an incredible succession of dishes which had been prepared by the wives of the peasants.

The tables literally groaned. We would start with antipasto, salamis, hams, stuffed pigs' heads, liver pâtés. Then followed a fragrant soup with home-made noodles. From the soup pot came a glorious pot-au-feu of chicken, rabbit, beef, pork and veal, onions, tomatoes, celery, and carrots.

Now was the time for heaping plates of spaghetti with meat sauce. A marvel of a sauce made from big chunks of meat, never from ground or chopped beef.

People laughed and kept on eating—fritto misto, roasted meats with sage-flavored potatoes that had been cooked in the drippings, fresh green salad, helpings of cheese, all washed down with Chianti. At the end there were fruit tarts and dried figs stuffed with nuts. The finale was a sweet Vino Santo.

It was this *ambiance* of relaxed jollity that I wanted to re-create at the Fair. For essentially we are friends who have come from many parts of the world to meet every two years in Florence.

Our first party took place at Marignolle. For seven hundred guests we tried to duplicate the Impruneta Fair as it was drawn and engraved by Jacques Callot in the seventeenth century. Itinerant rotisseurs from traveling fairs came to man the spits on which were roasted pigs and chickens. In the gardens overlooking Florence, we set up a merry-go-round and a shooting gallery. Men pedaling bicycle carts distributed ice cream. There were booths in which were made spun sugar candies and sweet anise wafers. Everybody had such a good time that we decided to make the Fair a season of parties and dinners and Florentine hospitality.

There were lunches for thirty or forty people. Some of the exhibitors also wanted to participate. The Genoese, the Milanese, the Neapolitans, the Venetians proudly prepared meals in their regional styles for the delight of the visitors from abroad.

For the 1963 Fair, we became even more ambitious. Florence was the birthplace of the Renaissance. Ergo, let us serve a series of Renaissance menus. For this undertaking which required great research as well as skill, I was fortunate enough to meet Giuseppe Maffioli, who has since become my great friend as well as my collaborator on a number of projects.

Maffioli is one of those felicitous phenomena which our peninsula occasionally seems to produce —the talented man of many parts. He is a stage director, an actor, a writer, a student, a *bon vivant*—and a gourmet. He comes from Treviso, an area of superlative cooking. When very young, to banish the boredom of solitary afternoons, he used to explore the family attic. Here he stumbled across a treasure of old gastronomic books and journals. His curiosity was aroused and he began to experiment with the orchestration of food, drawing forth subtle taste poems of flavors and perfumes.

Art has always been a selection. So the art of a gourmet is to refine away the excesses of gluttony, choosing with care the best of nature and harmonizing it into subtle savant preparations.

NOTE: *From the five Renaissance menus Maffioli and I presented at the 1963 Fair, we have selected recipes which will enable you to give two Renaissance dinners, no matter where you live. Herewith, the recipes are combined into two sample menus that could have been served in the Palazzo Strozzi in the days when the Strozzis were sitting down to table. Alongside the two sample menus for the American table we have given two of the actual menus from the '63 Fair.*

Renaissance Dinner
Menu I

## PALAZZO STROZZI
### *September 14, 1963*

*Menu I*

*Dinner given by the Committee of the third Mostra Internazionale dell'Antiquariato in honor of the exhibitors.*

VARIOUS COMPOSED SALADS WITH CAPERS AND ANCHOVIES
PICKLED MUSHROOMS

BROWN ONION SOUP
IMPERIAL SAFFRON SOUP

STEWED SHRIMPS
CISAME OF FISH WITH SWEET WHITE SAUCE

ONION OMELET PIE
TORTA MANFREDA

STUFFED CHICKEN
ROAST PIG WITH TARTAR SAUCE AND MUSTARD

FRUIT, NUNS' COOKIES,
PETITS FOURS   CANDIED CRAB APPLES
CAKE ON THE BALCONY
HIPPOCRATIC WINE

Please see *Note* page xi

VARIOUS MIXED SALADS WITH CAPERS
AND ANCHOVIES
CARABACCIA — BROWN ONION SOUP
STEWED SHRIMPS
MANFREDA TART
CHICKEN WITH FENNEL SEEDS
DESSERT OMELETS MEDICI
HIPPOCRATIC WINE

As far as we know, the carabaccia of the fourteenth century is one of the earliest existing versions of onion soup.
Later it passed to France where it underwent certain transformations to become the favorite restorative at *les Halles de Paris*.
The Renaissance carabaccia was a little too rich for modern tastes, so we reduced the amount of almonds and added broth to make a slightly more liquid soup.

## 1  Carabazada de magro

*Carabazada de magro*, as given by Cristoforo Messisbugo in "The Composition of Victuals" (fourteenth century).
Slice and peel the onions and cook well in water. Remove from water, drain well, put in a tin-lined pot, and boil them with one quart of good olive oil always stirring and mashing them.
Have one and a half pounds of ambrosine almonds well peeled and pounded into small bits, and cook over low heat with lemon juice, only long enough that they still retain their shape.
Place them in the same pot with half an ounce of cinnamon, and boil a little longer, always stirring.
When cooked and served, sprinkle with sugar and cinnamon.
After five centuries, we don't think there is anyone around who could take the combination of that much olive oil and cinnamon. The marriage of onions and almonds is something else again.

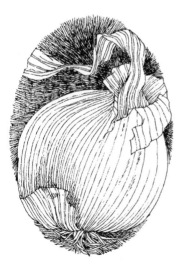

## 2  Carabaccia–Brown onion soup

Here is how Maffioli modernized this historic soup, emphasizing the two elements that we like best today.

Peel and chop the onions finely and the almonds.
Drop into the consommé.
Cover the pot and simmer over low heat for about 1 hour, by which time the onions should be reduced to rather a mush.
Pass the onions and almonds through a vegetable mill with the liquid to form a smooth thick soup.
Serve in a handsome tureen and top the soup with slices of bread which have been lightly fried on both sides in butter.
Sprinkle with a little freshly ground black pepper and a hearty dose of grated Parmesan.
If you want to add a touch of the classical tradition, omit the bread, pepper, and cheese and substitute a sprinkling of sugar and cinnamon.
Serves six.

6 medium onions
6 ounces blanched almonds
6 cups beef consommé
Bread
Butter
Pepper
Grated Parmesan cheese or
    sugar and cinnamon

## 3  Renaissance shrimps

This was a favorite banquet dish with rich Florentines of the Renaissance who liked to show they could afford to bring to their tables food from distant places. Pisa (which in those days was a busy commercial port on the Mediterranean, rivaling Genoa and Venice) is only fifty miles from Florence. However, for a horse cart it was a seven-hour journey. The precious load of fish and seafood was kept fresh with ice from the ice houses which were a luxury of the wealthy few.

*Shrimps as Prepared in the Renaissance.* Boil the shrimps. Remove the shells from the bodies, leaving the shrimps attached to the heads. Fry in a pan with fresh butter. Pour over a little vinegar, lemon juice, cinnamon, and pomegranate juice. Take from the pan and transfer to a lidded pot and let steam gently for a few minutes. Cover with a sauce made from flour, milk, butter, and soft bread crumbs. (This sauce was the antecedent of our present-day béchamel.)
We restyled *Savore di Gamberi* for the 1963 Florentine Antiques Fair.

## 4  *Savore di Gamberi – Stewed shrimps*

Flour the shrimps and sauté in the butter.
Add salt, pepper, cinnamon, and the raisins, which have been soaked in lemon or sour cherry juice until they are plump. Raisins and shrimps may sound startling, but together they produce a delicate exoticism which suggests the Orient.
Serve in barquettes.
Makes six servings.

2 tablespoons flour
1 pound peeled shrimp
Butter
Salt
Pepper
Dash of cinnamon
1 cup dried white raisins
Juice of 2 lemons or the equivalent
    of sour cherry juice

## 5  Manfreda tart

In a fourteenth-century cookbook, we discovered this baronial meat pasty, as full of surprises as four and twenty blackbirds baked in a pie. I am sure you will like manfreda, which is a kissing cousin to a quiche.

Prepare a baked 9-inch pie shell.
Sauté the diced salt pork in butter, until lightly browned.
Add the chopped chicken livers and cook, while stirring, for 3 minutes.
Add salt and pepper.
Sprinkle with wine and cook for 1 minute more.
Remove from fire and chop finely the livers and pork.
If the resulting mixture is too liquid, thicken with soft bread crumbs.
Add the Parmesan and well-beaten eggs.
Pour into pastry shell and bake in a moderate oven (350° F.) till set and a knife inserted in tart comes out clean.
Serves eight.

1 baked pie pastry shell
¼ pound lean salt pork
1 tablespoon butter
¾ pound chicken livers
Salt
Pepper
2 tablespoons white wine
1 slice soft white bread, crumbled
¼ cup grated Parmesan cheese
2 eggs

## 6  Chicken with fennel seeds

Florence has always loved the slightly anise flavor of fennel seeds. Fennel seeds give distinction to our adored sausage, *finocchiona*. In the fourteenth century, the cooks were already using fennel seeds to add excitement to the blandness of chicken.

Place chicken in pot and add water just to cover.
Boil slowly for 20 minutes.
Remove chicken.

1 3-pound broiler-fryer (cut in 8 pieces)
1 teaspoon fennel seeds
2 medium onions, minced
½ cup peeled minced almonds
¼ pound diced salt pork
Salt
Pepper

Add fennel seeds and onions to liquid in pot, and simmer until broth has been reduced by two-thirds.
Meanwhile in a frying pan, try out the diced salt pork.
Add almonds and chicken pieces and sauté until golden.
Pour on the broth.
Salt and pepper to taste.
Cook for 5 minutes and serve it forth.
Serves six.


## 7   Dessert omelets Medici

Several of the recipes may surprise you with their use of cinnamon, ginger, and other exciting spices. But you must remember the era.
Cinnamon, for example, was already prized in antique times, and is even cited in the Bible.
The Renaissance was passionate about cinnamon. And let's face it, cinnamon from Ceylon made a fortune for a number of Florentine merchant princes who were certainly not loath to promote its use. The more on the table, the more in the pocket.

½ cup white raisins
Juice of 2 oranges
6 eggs
Pinch of salt
4 tablespoons butter
1 tablespoon sugar
¼ teaspoon cinnamon
4 tablespoons curaçao

Soak the raisins in the orange juice for about an hour.
Beat eggs with pinch of salt.
Make twelve little omelets, cooking three at a time in ½ tablespoon of butter.
When they are done, put a few soaked raisins in each omelet.
Sprinkle surface with sugar and cinnamon.
Roll up and arrange side by side in a buttered ovenware dish.
Pour over curaçao and place in moderate oven (350° F.) for 10 minutes.
Serves six.

## 8  Hippocratic Wine

The Greek physician Hippocrates (460–360 B.C.) is regarded as the Father of Medicine. If Hippocrates recommended it, it was good for you. Since he lived to be 100 years old, have no fears when you quaff a glass of hot Hippocratic wine. It would be even more wonderful taken from a silver goblet.

In the fourteenth century, you were advised to start with the finest red wine obtainable and the best of all honey.

We suggest you follow the same principles today.

4 cups red Chianti
½ cup honey
1 stick cinnamon
Zest of 1 lemon
12 cloves

Combine all ingredients in a saucepan.
Boil slowly all together until the mixture is reduced by ⅓.
While a little is good, more is not necessarily better.

Renaissance Dinner
Menu II

*September 21, 9:00* P.M.

*Meat and fish dinner given by the Associazione Antiquari d'Italia and by Giuseppe and Mario Bellini in honor of the participators at the third Mostra Internazionale dell'Antiquariato. The following dishes were served under the arches and in the gardens of the Villa Bellini at Marignolle:*

Please see *Note* page xi

MUSHROOM PIE

IMPERIAL SAFFRON SOUP

BLASMANGERI

FISH IN GARLIC SAUCE

MARINATED WILD BOAR

ROAST CAPON À L'ORANGE

MALMONA — RICE PIE AROMATIZED
    WITH ORANGE

VARIOUS MIXED SALADS WITH MUSHROOMS AND TUNA FISH

FISH WITH SAPOR BIANCO

MARINATED EEL

WILD BOAR

BRAWN

VARIOUS SALAMI-STUFFED SAUSAGES

TRIPE POTACCHIO

ASPARAGUS SOUP WITH SAFFRON, PINE KERNELS, AND PISTACHIO NUTS

TWICE-BOILED SOUP

RICE WITH VARIOUS DRESSINGS

TREDURA

MUSHROOM TART

FRANCESCA CAKE

DUCK WITH ORANGE SAUCE

MARINATED WILD BOAR

ROASTED CHICKEN WITH FENNEL SEEDS

VARIOUS FRUITS

CENCI, QUINQUINELLI, PIGNOCCATE, PETITS FOURS, DOLZETTI
    AND MARZIPAN

HIPPOCRATIC WINE

## 9 Mushroom pie

Tuscany has always been a region rich with wild mushrooms. Some of them grow as big as toadstools and people have been known to broil a single mushroom cap as if it were a steak. For centuries, these exquisite wild mushrooms have graced the tables of peasant and prince.

Cover the bottom of a heavy skillet with the olive oil.
Sauté the mushrooms with the bacon, garlic, and parsley.
Remove from fire and cool.
Add Parmesan, eggs, salt, and pepper.
Mix together and pour into a pie pan lined with pie pastry.
Bake in a moderate oven (350° F.) until the eggs are set and the pastry is nut-colored.
This mushroom tart makes a good main course for a light lunch as well as an opening for a formal dinner.

3 tablespoons olive oil
1 pound chopped mushrooms
6 slices bacon diced
2 cloves garlic, minced
2 tablespoons minced parsley
1 cup diced Parmesan cheese
4 eggs
Salt
Pepper
Pastry for single-crust 9-inch pie

## 10  Imperial saffron soup

Saffron comes from the Persian word for crocus, *zahfaran*. The Moors introduced it to Spain from whence it passed through Europe. The dried and crushed stigmata of the flower have always been expensive. Thus, quite naturally, any dish flavored with saffron became known as Imperial.

Cut into julienne strips the breast of one boiled chicken, or preferably a capon.
Slice the almonds lengthwise.
Add the pine nuts and mix all together.
Drop into the broth.
(An Imperial cook would have made his soup from scratch but you can obtain excellent results with a quality canned chicken broth.)
Boil for 5 minutes.
Introduce the sherry.
Remove from the fire and add the saffron, the pinch of cinnamon, and the egg yolks which have been beaten with the cream.
The result will be smooth, unctuous, and royal.
Serves six.

1 boiled chicken breast
¾ cup almonds, shelled, blanched
and skinned
2 tablespoons pine nuts
6 cups chicken broth
½ cup sherry
Pinch of saffron
Pinch of cinnamon
2 egg yolks
½ cup cream

## 11  Blasmangeri

The *blasmangeri* is an ancestor of the modern *risotto*.

Try out the diced bacon.
Add the minced onion and sauté together slowly.
When the onion is pale gold, toss in the rice and stir well for 2 or 3 minutes.

6 slices diced bacon
½ white onion, minced
¾ cup rice
⅓ cup white wine
2 cups chicken broth

12

Sprinkle on the white wine.

As soon as it has evaporated, add warmed chicken broth, a little at a time.

You must be conscientious about stirring constantly, or the rice will stick.

The whole process results in a thick creamy rice.

It will take 20 to 30 minutes.

A few minutes before it is ready to remove from the fire, add the pepper, nutmeg, Parmesan, and cream.

Mix together with love until all the ingredients are well amalgamated.

Serve immediately in heated plates.

Serves six.

Pepper
Nutmeg
2 tablespoons grated Parmesan cheese
4 tablespoons cream

## 12  Fish in garlic sauce

Lay the sole in a broad shallow pan with the bay leaves and the lemon slices.

Pour on dry white wine to cover.

Simmer gently for 15 minutes.

Remove from pan.

Skin and bone the fish, and lay the fillets on a heated platter.

(You can simplify your life by poaching the fillets only, but the flavor is more pronounced when you have cooked your fish whole.)

Prepare your sauce in advance or if you are very rapid while the sole is cooking.

Boil the eggs and the garlic cloves for 7 minutes.

(Boiled garlic is less strong, but nonetheless there will be enough

6 sole
2 bay leaves
1 lemon, sliced
White wine

2 eggs
2 cloves garlic
2 slices bread
Juice and grated zest of 1 lemon
Salt
Pepper
1 cup olive oil

garlic taste to subtly perfume the sauce.)
Put the hardboiled eggs and garlic through a food mill with the
bread from which you have trimmed away the crusts.
Add the lemon juice and zest, salt, and pepper.
Slowly incorporate the oil drop by drop, beating well.
Pour the sauce over the fillets of sole, which have been kept
warm, and serve as quickly as possible.
Serves six.

## 13   Marinated wild boar

The swampy forest lands of the Maremma, the formerly wild
coast between Rome and Pisa, abounded in boar which were
highly appreciated by the Florentines. Sportsmen still hunt for boar
in this area, although the supply today is much diminished. Those
who live in more civilized parts of the world, where this delicacy
is not obtainable, can use our recipe to excellent results by
substituting lean loin of pork.

2 pounds lean boar or pork loin
Dry red wine for marinade
Flour
1 pound onions, chopped
Olive oil
Salt
Cayenne pepper
1 cup Marsala
½ pound diced ripe quince
Beef consommé

Cut the meat into 1-inch cubes and cover with red wine for three
days.
(For pork, one day would be sufficient.)
Remove meat from marinade and dry each piece thoroughly.
Flour the meat cubes.
Sauté the onions in olive oil until pale gold.
Add the meat and turn constantly until browned.
Season with salt and cayenne.
Pour on the marsala and add the diced quince.
The tartness of the quince produces the famous Italian *agrodolce,*
a mild sweet-and-sour flavor.

Place all the ingredients, including the red wine marinade, in a
Dutch oven (or flameproof earthenware casserole) with a tight-
fitting lid.
Simmer gently for 1 hour.
Remove lid and continue cooking over a low flame for an
additional hour.
If the meat becomes dry, add a little heated beef consommé.
Serves six.

## 14 Roast capon à l'orange

Duck *à l'orange* really didn't originate with *La Tour d'Argent*.
Italy is a country where oranges grow. People tend to use what
they have around them. Cooking with oranges has been part of
our gastronomic tradition for centuries, long before François I and
Charles VIII took Italian food specialties back to amaze the
French courts.
The following recipe can be beautifully adapted to chicken, duck,
duckling, baby turkey, and pheasant as well as capon. It was one
of the festive dishes of the Medicis. Rich Romans, according to
Martial, were terribly partial to duck. It is quite possible that the
Caesars were already eating it with oranges.
This was the style of Renaissance Florence as it appeared in a
book of the period:
"Take a good cold boiled capon. If the capon is roasted, no
matter. Cut into small pieces and toss into a skillet with a half
pound of butter or fat and fry very well. When the capon is well
fried, throw on the juice of ten oranges, sugar and cinnamon."
We adapted this mouth-watering dish for the 1963 fair as follows:

Bard the capon with bacon slices.

Roast in moderate oven (350° F.) approximately 30 minutes per pound.

(Duck would take 2 to 2½ hours. Pheasant and chicken would require only 1 to 1½ hours.)

When the bacon is browned, pour over the bird one cup of dry white wine.

Baste regularly with the juices thereafter.

Soak bread, crusts removed, in the juice of 6 oranges.

Pass through a food mill.

Add the grated orange zest, cinnamon, ginger, pepper, cloves, and saffron.

Add ½ cup dry white wine to the roasting juices in the pan, and add the mixture of bread and spices, the raisins, and the half cup of wine in which the raisins have been soaked.

Cut the capon into 8 sections.

Place in an oval ovenproof casserole, just large enough to compactly contain the bird.

Cover with the sauce, and heat for 5 to 10 minutes.

Serves six.

1 capon (6 to 8 pounds)
8 to 10 thin slices bacon
1 cup dry white wine
Juice of 6 oranges
2 slices white bread
Zest of 1 orange, grated
Pinch of ground cinnamon
Pinch of ground ginger
Pinch of pepper
Pinch of ground cloves
Pinch of saffron
2 tablespoons raisins soaked in
    ½ cup white wine

## 15  Malmona

Rice pudding has been made for a long time. Probably because we were subjected to the pap of the nursery-room version, we have never become addicts. However, this palace style of rice pudding—as you will see—can go to any black tie dinner.

Rinse the rice well under running cold water to remove the starch.
Cook the rice in the milk until soft and creamy.
Force through a food mill or sieve.
Beat the eggs with the sugar or honey and add to the rice along with the melted butter, 1 teaspoon orange blossom water, and the candied orange peel.
Mix well.
Butter a soufflé mold.
Pour in the mixture and set the dish in a pan of warm water.
Bake in a moderate oven (350° F.) for 25 minutes.
Serve warm with a hot sauce made by heating marmalade with 1 teaspoon orange blossom water.
Serves six.

¾ cup rice
4 cups milk
5 eggs
2 cups sugar or honey
¼ pound butter, melted
2 teaspoons orange blossom water
½ pound diced candied orange peel
1 cup orange marmalade

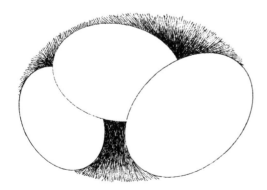

Menus from the Fifth Fair

## THE COURTYARD OF PALAZZO STROZZI
### September 21, 1967

*Dinner in Honor of the Exhibitors at the 5th Biennale dell'Antiquariato*

Menu dedicated to Vincenzo Corrado. Recipes adapted from *Il Cuoco Galante* published in Naples in 1778.

COLD HORS D'OEUVRE OF TOMATOES

TIMBALE RIGATONI

FISH GALANTINE

    WITH SAUCE ALLA VICENZINA

LEMON AND TOMATO SHERBET

STUFFED TOMATOES:

    WITH HERBS

    CORRADINA STYLE

    WITH RICE

    NEAPOLITAN STYLE

    CULATTA DI MONGANA

    WITH SAUCE CORRADINA STYLE

SPINACH AND CELERY

CAKE CORRADINA STYLE

WINE: CAPRI AND SALERNO

LIQUORI STOCK — CHAMPAGNE MERCIER

Cooks: *Lauro Giraldi — Marino Dona — Nino Marino*
Pastry-cooks: *Oswaldo Bettucci — Otello Ferroni*

TIMBALE RIGATONI

FISH GALLANTINE WITH SAUCE ALLA

    VICENZINA

LEMON AND TOMATO SHERBET

COULIS OF TOMATO

CAKE CORRADINA STYLE

For the Fair of 1967, we were inspired by great chefs of the past like the Italians Vincenzo Corrado and Federico Grandi, and the Frenchman Antoine Carême.

Vincenzo Corrado was a paradoxical character. He was both the abbot of a Neapolitan monastery and an inventive cook of scholarly mind. In 1778 appeared a classified volume of his experiments in the kitchen, entitled "The Gallant Cook."

It was full of innovations. He suggested to the gentry to incorporate the good regional cooking of the common people.

He established the tomato as an element of gastronomy. (At the same time in France, Parmentier was urging the many uses of the potato.)

The Bourbons, reigning family of Naples, adopted the tomato with enthusiasm. From them, it passed to their royal relatives around Europe. Corrado was wild with imagination. He employed the tomato in sauces, in sherbets, in cakes.

As a divertissement at our dinner in honor of Corrado, the Ballet Company of Florence danced out a portrait of the "golden apple" (pomodoro) of the vegetable world from the time of its discovery to its presentation at court.

## 16   Timbale rigatoni

Chop finely the carrot, onion, celery, parsley, and the prosciutto. Sauté lightly in 1 tablespoon of olive oil and 1 tablespoon of butter in a Dutch oven.

Disjoint, wash and dry oxtail.

Cube the beef and pork.

Place the meats in the Dutch oven and brown, stirring and turning with a wooden spoon so the meat does not stick to the skillet.

When well browned, pour in the wine and cook gently until it evaporates.

Now add enough water to cover all the meat in the casserole.

Salt and pepper to taste.

Put a well-fitting lid on the Dutch oven.

Cook over low flame for 2 hours.

Remove meat from the casserole.

Stir in the tomato paste, 1 tablespoon olive oil, 1 tablespoon butter.

Cook for 10 to 15 minutes. Strain sauce and put aside for the moment.

Remove the meat from the oxtail and put through meat grinder with the pork and beef.

Mix with the ricotta cheese, and the béchamel sauce.

Line a deep mold with basic pie crust.

Add a layer of parboiled *rigatoni*, which have been filled with the mixture of meat, cheese, and béchamel.

Alternate with a layer of the sauce, and a dusting of Parmesan.

Continue to the top of the mold and seal with a pie crust.

Pierce crust with the prongs of a fork and brush the surface with beaten egg yolk which gives the pastry an attractive golden color.

Bake for 20 minutes, or until the crust is nicely browned.

Serve with tomato sauce (Coulis of tomato).

Makes eight to ten servings.

2 tablespoons butter
2 tablespoons olive oil
1 carrot
1 onion
1 stalk celery
1 sprig parsley
½ pound prosciutto, diced
1 oxtail
½ pound lean beef
½ pound lean pork
½ cup red wine
Salt
Pepper
2 tablespoons tomato paste
2 cups ricotta cheese
2 cups béchamel flavored with
 ¼ teaspoon nutmeg and
 ⅓ cup grated Parmesan cheese
1 basic pie crust
1½ pounds *rigatoni*
1 egg yolk

## 17  Coulis of tomato

(This is the first recipe for tomato sauce ever to have appeared in any cookbook. It is vague but interesting.)
"Ripe tomatoes are cooked in the fat pared away from raw ham and flavored with a little garlic, basil, a bay leaf, salt, and pepper. Bathe with an excellent broth. Bring to a boil adding toasted bread crusts. When everything has been cooked to a pulp, pass through a sieve."

Beppe swears he can produce this extravaganza from start to finish in three hours. "After all, what do you do with all the time while the meat is cooking?" Nothing. Just make pie crust, tomato sauce, cook the *rigatoni* and wait.
I think it would take me three days. The onerous stuffing of the *rigatoni*, Beppe does deftly by inserting the farce with a pointed demitasse spoon. A pastry bag with a large nozzle might simplify the job.
This timbale is certainly nothing for a non-initiate to tackle without plenty of time. However, should you make the effort, your friends will never forget you. If they do, drop them immediately.
I would short cut some of the pain by substituting *cannelloni* for the *rigatoni* because the sheets of dough can be easily rolled around the filling. Corrado may have made history but he probably had an enormous staff of kitchen helpers.

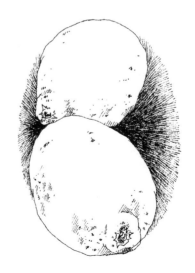

## 18  Lemon and tomato sherbet

The idea of ices probably came to the Italians from the Chinese. Just another reward from the celebrated voyage of Marco Polo. In the sixteenth century the Italians introduced ices to the rest of

Europe through marriage. When Catherine de Medici became the bride of Henry II of France, part of her dowry included a retinue of Florentine cooks.

In the eighteenth century, Corrado had the felicitous idea of creating a sherbet of lemon and tomato juices to be served midway through a groaning banquet as a palate clearer. Thus refreshed, the *bon-vivants* of his time were ready to take on another half-dozen courses.

(Ices and sherbets, like ice creams, may be frozen in refrigerator trays; but like ice cream, they need beating for smoothness and are better made in a freezer. If the sherbet is made in the refrigerator, beat it thoroughly every half-hour during the freezing. In either case, let the finished sherbet stand, well-guarded against melting, to mellow for a few hours.)

Add sugar to water and boil for 5 minutes.

Let cool.

Mix lemon juice with the sugar water.

Place ⅔ of lemon juice mixture in the ice cream freezer and churn until half-thickened.

Add the beaten white of one egg which will give a more sparkling appearance to the mixture.

Continue churning until proper consistency.

Remove from freezer.

Place in a covered container and keep in freezing compartment of refrigerator.

To the remaining ⅓ lemon juice and sugar water, add an equivalent quantity of tomato juice.

Pour in ice cream freezer and churn until the right consistency.

To serve, place in individual glass bowls, one scoop of lemon sherbet and one scoop of tomato sherbet.

½ cup sugar
2 cups water
Juice of 10 lemons
1 egg white
Tomato juice (about 1½ cups)

The two colors make a pretty contrast and the taste is most
pleasing and light on the tongue.
Serves six.


## 19 *Fish galantine with sauce alla Vicenzina*

Corrado's fish galantine is a wonderful summer dish. It can be
prepared well in advance in the cool of the morning and is
especially suitable for dining on a terrace when you would like
something special that offers no last minute problems in serving.

Take the fish and marinate for at least 12 hours in dry white wine
with bay leaves, parsley, celery, fennel leaves, and lemon peel.
Prepare a farce made from pounded or blended fillet of sole, tuna
fish in oil, chopped aromatic herbs and eggs.
Fill the boned and marinated fish with this farce and coat with
shelled pistachio nuts.
Wrap in gauze or cheesecloth and boil for an hour in the wine
marinade diluted with court bouillon.
(Carefully skim the stock.)
Allow the fish to cool in the broth to which the gelatin has been
added.
When an aspic has been formed, remove the gauze and cut the
fish into slices.
Serve with a little of the jelly and Vicenzina sauce.

Sauce: Pound together capers, garlic, truffles, parsley, basil
and boil in a little quantity of court bouillon with dry white
wine, lemon, and vinegar.
Reduce and add black pepper and olive oil.
Serve cold.

Any firm-fleshed fish (tuna, halibut,
    sea bass, cod, or salmon)
Dry white wine
Bay leaves
Parsley
Celery
Fennel leaves
Lemon peel
Fillet of sole
Tuna in oil
Pistachio nuts
Chopped aromatic herbs
Eggs
1 envelope unflavored gelatin

## LUNCHEON IN THE REFECTORY

## OF THE CISTERCIAN ABBEY OF GALLUZZO
*September 26, 1967*

So renowned were the eighteenth-century cooks of Italy that they were called upon by the leading monarchs of Europe.

Menu dedicated to Francesco Leonardi, Roman cook formerly in the service of Her Imperial Highness Catherine II of Russia.

NETTLE OR LUPPERI SOUP

ROAST TURKEY

WITH PEAVRADA SAUCE

ENDIVE AND LETTUCE ALLA ROPESCE

BRAINS MONGANA

COULIS OF SHRIMPS

LAMB CUTLET ALLA CAPPUCCINA

LITTLE BASKETS OF PASTRY

AUTUMN FRUITS

WINE AND SPIRITS MADE BY THE MONKS OF THE CERTOSA

Cook: Nino Marino

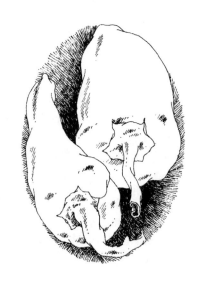

## LUNCHEON IN HONOR
## OF THE ACCADEMIA ITALIANA DELLA CUCINA
## IN PALAZZO STROZZI  *September 18, 1967*

During the nineteenth century, one of the richest families of
Russia was Demidoff. They chose to live abroad in Florence. The
Villa Demidoff, filled with incomparable art treasures, was a center
of Florentine social life for decades.
(Recently the house and its contents were sold at auction by
Sotheby's.) Our lunch of September 18 was dedicated to the
Demidoff chef, Federico Grandi.

CREAM OF PEA SOUP

ASPIC OF FILLETS DE SOLES À LA RAVIGOTTE

SAUTÉ OF FILLETS OF PARTRIDGE WITH TRUFFLES

BOHEMIAN ROAST

GATEAU CONDÉ WITH STRAWBERRY JELLY

CHOCOLATE AND VANILLA ICE CREAM


WINES:

VAL D'ARBIA BIANCO DI CASA RICASOLI

GRIGNANO DI CASA GONDI

VIN SANTO DI CASA FRESCOBALDI


Prepared by Doney
Cook: Lauro Giraldi

# THE MASKED BALL DINNER   *October 14, 1967*

Marie-Antoine (Antonin) Carême (1784–1833) was the chef of
Prince Talleyrand for twelve years. He then spread his talents
around Europe, heading important kitchens in St. Petersburg,
London, Vienna, before returning to France in the service of Baron
James de Rothschild. His learned treatises on the art of cooking
provided the first solid base for the development of La Cuisine
Française.

Menu dedicated to the famous Carême.

HAM À LA FINANCIÈRE

SOUP OF ASPARAGUS TIPS

HORLY DE FILLETS DE SOLES

RAGOUT D'ESCALOPES DE HOMARD À LA NAVARIN

FOIE GRAS AND TRUFFLES AU SUPRÊME

SOUFFLÉ OF CHICKEN

BEEF PIQUÉ, MARINADE ROEBUCK

POTATO CROQUETTES

WHIPPED CREAM AU MARASQUIN

GENOISE À L'ORANGE


WINES: BLANC DE BLANC

CHIANTI ANTINORI AND CHIANTI GUICCIARDINI


Dinner prepared by the *Istituto* Professionale Alberghiero di Stato
"Aurelio Saffi," Florence.
Teacher-cook: Pasquale Alberti
Teacher-pastry-cook: Otello Perroni

*September 30, 10* P.M.

Long before there was a unified Italy, our country was a mosaic
of ducal regions and city-states. Each had its own individual court,
customs, culture, and cooking.
On September 30 a dinner was given by the Associazione
Antiquari d'Italia and by Giuseppe and Mario Bellini in honor of
the exhibitors at the Quinta Mostra Internazionale
dell'Antiquariato and dedicated to regional Italian cooking. It was
served under the arches in the gardens and in the cellars of the
Bellini Villa at Marignolle.

ITALIAN GASTRONOMIC RHAPSODY

| | |
|---|---|
| *Piedmont:* | Stracotto al Barolo (Beef stew with wine) |
| *Lombardy:* | Minestrone – Tripe alla Milanese |
| *Veneto:* | Pasta and beans – Baccalà alla Vicentina with Polenta |
| *Liguria:* | Thin noodles with pesto – Stuffed cold veal alla Genovese |
| *Emilia:* | Tagliatelle alla Bolognese – Zamponi (Stuffed pigs' trotters) Cotechini (Pork sausage) with purée of potatoes |
| *Tuscany:* | Pappa of tomatoes – Chicken all'arrabbiata Beans all'uccelletto |
| *Latium:* | Penne all'Amatrice – Roast baby lamb |
| *Campania:* | Spaghetti alle vongole – Pizze |
| *Puglia:* | Purée of beans and chicory |
| *Sicily:* | Caponata (Eggplant and anchovy appetizer) |
| *Sardinia:* | Roast pork |

Wines:      Soave and Valpolicella Folonari (Veneto)
Bianco Lugana and Riva Garda Folonari (Lombardy)
Rosatello and Chianti Ruffino Riserva Ducale 1961
(Tuscany)
Orvieto Ruffino (Lazio)

## 20  *Minestrone alla Milanese*

In Italy, minestrone essentially is the vegetable garden thrown into a soup pot. There are dozens of recipes and all of them are authentic. Every five miles and you will get another kind of minestrone.

Soak beans overnight.
Cook in salted water for 45 minutes.
Drain.
Try out the pork or bacon.
Add the butter.
Stir in the leeks, carrots, cabbage, celery, spinach, potatoes, basil, parsley.
Season with salt and pepper.
After 5 minutes, add the tomatoes, the beans, and the stock.
Cook slowly for 2 hours.
Now add the rice and the sausages.
Continue simmering for another 15 minutes, when rice will be done.
At end, stir in the grated Parmesan.
Remove sausages.
Slice them and return to soup.
Serve broth and vegetables in large handsome pottery tureen.
Serves eight.

2 pounds dried white beans
½ cup diced salt pork or bacon
3 tablespoons butter
2 leeks, chopped (if unobtainable, use 2 yellow onions, chopped)
2 carrots, peeled and chopped
½ head small white cabbage, shredded
⅓ cup diced celery
½ pound spinach leaves
2 potatoes, peeled and diced
2 tablespoons basil
2 tablespoons parsley
1 tablespoon salt
½ teaspoon pepper
2 tomatoes, peeled and chopped
8 cups chicken stock
¾ cup uncooked rice
2 pork sausages
6 tablespoons grated Parmesan cheese

## 21 Stuffed cold veal

The bustling, noisy port of Genoa today attracts few tourists. The food of the city, however, deserves much attention. This is one of Genoa's specialties, adored in the small *trattorie* and generally snubbed by the big restaurants and the great hotels. Because the *cima* is prepared in advance and served cold, it is a splendid addition to a home buffet. At Simposio 67, the Genovese got a big hand for this one, which is well worth the work involved.

Soak the brain in warm salted water to clean it of skin, blood, and filaments.
Prepare the sweetbreads by soaking for 15 minutes in icy water acidulated with the lemon juice.
Trim away all membranes.
Blanch the brain and sweetbreads together in the same water.
Cut the leg of veal into small pieces.
Sauté in 4 tablespoons butter with the cut-up brain and sweetbreads.
Mince fine.
Soak the dried mushrooms until they swell up.
Dry well to remove excess water.
In a large bowl, combine the uncooked peas, pistachio nuts, minced garlic, marjoram, mushrooms, Parmesan, the minced veal, brain, and sweetbreads, salt and pepper.
Beat well the 6 eggs and add to the mixture.
Flatten the veal breast until it is ¼ inch thick.
Fold over and sew up the two sides so that you have a neat bag into which to place the above stuffing.
Fill two-thirds full.
In cooking, the meat tends to shrink and the stuffing swells.

½ calf brain
2 pounds boned veal breast
¼ pound lean leg of veal
1 pound sweetbreads
Juice of 1 lemon
1 cup dried mushrooms
1 cup shelled green peas
2 tablespoons pistachio nuts
2 cloves garlic, minced
½ teaspoon marjoram
4 heaping tablespoons grated
    Parmesan cheese
6 tablespoons butter
2 tablespoons oil
½ cup dry white wine
6 eggs
Salt
Pepper
1 carrot
1 stalk celery
1 onion

Sew up the top of the pocket.
Brown the meat on all sides in a Dutch oven, using 2 tablespoons butter and 2 tablespoons of oil.
Add dry white wine; let evaporate.
Add water to cover, introducing a carrot, a stalk of celery, and an onion into the pot.
Turn meat occasionally.
Simmer for 2 hours.
Remove from Dutch oven and let cool.
Cover with grease-proof paper and a heavy weight to compress the meat and the stuffing.
Remove the thread and cut the meat into slices.
Serve well chilled but not too cold.
Serves twelve.

## 22   Pappa of tomatoes

In the old days in the country districts of Tuscany, it was the custom to bake bread once a week only. By the end of the week, the bread had become stale. However, the peasants were too thrifty to throw it away. To use it, they devised *panzanella* and *pappa al pomodoro*. The talented frugality of Tuscan peasants has given us these two tasty dishes which today are the delight of all Florentines.

Sauté the onion in the olive oil until pale gold.
Add the tomatoes and the tomato paste.
Stir and simmer for 20 minutes.
Meanwhile put the bread, which has been broken into small pieces, the garlic, the basil, and water into a deep saucepan.

1 onion (thinly sliced)
5 tablespoons olive oil
1 cup peeled tomatoes
2 tablespoons tomato paste
Stale Italian bread
3 cloves garlic
10 leaves sweet basil (or 1 tablespoon dry)
7 cups water
1 tablespoon salt
½ tablespoon pepper
Olive oil

Cook and stir over a low flame until the mixture becomes a thick smooth mush.
Add salt and pepper, and the onion-tomato sauce.
Amalgamate the two by beating well with a whisk.
The result is a thick soup.
Each person at table pours a little fresh olive oil on the top of his portion.
(This is a filling dish, but it is supposed to be.)
Serves eight.

## 23 Panzanella

The *pappa al pomodoro* was eaten in the farmhouses for supper. The *panzanella* is a cold dish which is carried as a picnic lunch in the fields. The ingredients are put together at the last minute. At home, the peasants soaked the bread in water and squeezed it out well in a clean cloth. This was carried along to the fields and kept in the shade. The tomatoes and cucumbers were simply picked on the spot from the vines. Everything is put together at the last minute. Beppe finds it a refreshing salad and his guests have made it one of his most popular summer dishes.

(Country bread—compact in texture and slightly gray in color—is a staple in Italy and France.
In America, you would probably have to use whole wheat bread or sour rye.)
Cut the bread into thick rough slices and trim away the crusts.
Soak the dry slices in ice cold water.
Crumble well with your hands until you get soggy pellets.
Squeeze well in a clean cloth, extracting all the moisture.

1 pound stale Italian whole wheat bread
¼ cup olive oil
2 tablespoons vinegar
1 teaspoon salt
½ teaspoon pepper
4 to 5 spring onions or 1 large onion, sliced
1 cucumber sliced
10 leaves basil
4 ripe tomatoes

By now your bread is edible bread again.
Place the bundle in the refrigerator for several hours.
This will dry out the bread even further, and give the desirable coldness.
Make a dressing by mixing well the olive oil, vinegar, salt, and pepper.
In a salad bowl, put the onions, the slices of cucumber, quantities of fragrant basil, and the bread.
At the moment of serving, add the tomato wedges and the dressing.
Toss well.
Serves eight.

## 24  White beans uccelletto

We don't know why these beans are called "in the style of a little bird," except that when you taste them, your spirits soar.
There is a popular rhyme in Florence, which loosely translated goes something like this: "Florentines in front of white beans lick their plates and their napkins too."
Because this dish is truly rooted in the popular culture, there are as many ways of making it as there are housewives in Tuscany.
Beppe is no housewife, but this is his version.

1 pound white beans
3 tablespoons whole sage leaves
½ cup peeled tomatoes
2 tablespoons tomato paste
¼ cup olive oil
2 cloves garlic
Salt
Pepper
6 or 7 Italian pork sausages

Soak the beans in water overnight.
Drain and place in an earthenware bean pot with the sage, the peeled tomatoes, tomato paste, olive oil, and garlic.
Add water just to cover.
Cover with lid.
Set in an oven pre-heated to 350° F.

After 30 minutes, lower the heat to 250° F.
From time to time, stir with a wooden spoon.
The cooking will take 3 to 4 hours.
During the last hour, check the liquid.
Add hot water when necessary.
Salt and pepper when almost cooked.
Boil the sausages in a frying pan with water just to cover.
This removes the fat.
Boil until water has practically evaporated.
Add sausages to the bean pot during the last 30 minutes of cooking.
Serves twelve.

## 25  Roast spring lamb with new potatoes

For the *Simposio*, the Romans came with one of their favorite spaghetti dishes and with the roast spring baby lamb that has become almost synonymous with their city.
At Easter, Roman friends send Beppe a present of a whole lamb. They feel their pasture gives lamb a flavor which cannot be duplicated elsewhere. Even though all of us are not so well gifted, this recipe makes a terrific party dish out of any spring lamb.

Wipe lamb with damp cloth.
Rub meat with garlic and a little olive oil; sprinkle inside and out with salt and pepper.
Make a series of slits and insert slivers of garlic and rosemary.
Roast in moderate oven (350° F.) for 2½ hours.
Turn occasionally.

1 baby lamb (about 8 pounds, ready to cook)
2 large cloves garlic
Olive oil
Salt
Pepper
1 teaspoon rosemary
½ cup dry red wine
3 pounds small new potatoes, peeled and cut in half

After 10 minutes, baste with the wine.
Thereafter baste with the pan juices.
After 1 hour, surround the lamb with the potatoes which have been salted and peppered.
Be sure to turn the potatoes from time to time, so they become nicely browned.
Serve the lamb and potatoes without the pan juices, which have absorbed most of the fat from the lamb.
Serves eight to ten.

## 26   Spaghetti with clams, Neapolitan style

With more than five thousand miles of coastline, much of it sandy, Italy has never suffered from a shortage of clams. It is only natural that Italians dreamed up clam sauce to go on their spaghetti. Naples, with its penchant for tomatoes, adds tomatoes to the sauce. Beppe prefers his clam sauce white. Both ways are equally delicious: According to local tradition, you never sprinkle cheese on *spaghetti alle vongole*. Or on any other fish or shellfish, for that matter. Iconoclasts, of course, break the rules.

Scrub fresh clams under cold running water to remove all sand and grit.
Place in deep skillet with ½ cup water.
Cover and steam until opened.
Discard shells, strain and keep liquid.
If canned clams are used, drain and reserve juice.
Heat oil in saucepan.
Stir in garlic and onion.
After 1 minute remove garlic, add tomatoes, salt, pepper, oregano, and clam juice.

2 pounds small hard-shelled clams (or 2 cans whole clams)
½ cup water
4 tablespoons olive oil
2 cloves garlic, minced
1 onion, chopped
1½ pounds ripe tomatoes, peeled and chopped (or 1 1-pound can Italian peeled tomatoes)
Salt
Pepper
½ teaspoon oregano
2 tablespoons minced parsley
1 pound spaghetti, cooked and drained

Cook over low heat for 30 minutes.
Add parsley and clams.
Cook 2 minutes only.
Pour over hot drained spaghetti.
Serves six.


## 27   *Caponata alla siciliana*

In Sicily the spicy *caponata* is a staple that appears in every household. It is used mainly for an hors d'oeuvre, but it might also appear as a side dish or spread on bread for a snack. You can make it in large quantities, for it keeps well in a refrigerator for two weeks.

Peel the eggplants and slice lengthwise.
Salt and leave for 30 minutes until the eggplants have given up their water.
Wash and dry well and sauté eggplant slices in ⅓ cup olive oil until browned on both sides.
Remove and drain on absorbent paper.
Slice lengthwise the hearts of celery, taking care to leave the stalks attached at the bottom.
They will then resemble bows, according to one fanciful Italian.
Add the rest of the oil to the skillet and fry the celery.
Drain on the absorbent paper, alongside the eggplant slices.
Parboil the peeled small white onions.
Drain, dry and sauté them in olive oil until they take on a pale gold color.
Sprinkle with sugar and stir carefully as they brown.
Add the vinegar, salt and pepper and cook until the vinegar has been reduced to half its quantity.

4 or 5 eggplants
⅔ cup olive oil
¼ pound hearts of celery
½ pound small white onions, peeled
¼ cup sugar
½ cup white wine vinegar
1 teaspoon salt
¼ teaspoon pepper
1 pound ripe tomatoes,
    peeled and seeded
½ cup diced black olives
2 tablespoons capers
2 tablespoons pine nuts or sliced
    almonds
1 tablespoon chopped parsley

Cut the tomatoes in quarters and add to onions.
Simmer for 20 minutes, adding water if necessary.
Return the eggplant and the celery to the pan.
Add the olives, the capers, the nuts, and the chopped parsley.
Simmer just long enough for all the ingredients to be heated up together.
Remove from pan and chill.
The *caponata* should be prepared well in advance so that the ingredients absorb the sweet-and-sour flavor of the tomatoes.
*Caponata* is particularly attractive when served in a dome shape; surrounded with a garnish of tuna fish, hard-boiled eggs and shrimps.

Lunch Prepared by
the Milanese Exhibitors

The Milanese have been jealous all through their history. When they saw what we were doing at the Fair, they could not bear it and begged me if they could prepare a Milanese style lunch in the courtyard of Marignolle. I was delighted.

I knew I could count on this crowd. They surpassed my expectations. They even made a special trip to Milan to get the *ossibuchi* and the cutlets from their favorite butcher. (They trusted no one else.)

The following dishes were made by Fiorella Gerosa, the daughter of Luciano Gerosa, the Milan dealer in antique carpets.

RISOTTO ALLA MILANESE

OSSIBUCHI ALLA MILANESE

VEAL CUTLETS MILANESE

VEGETABLE

DESSERT

## 28  Ossibuchi alla Milanese

Sauté the onion in the butter until golden brown.
Flour the veal knuckles and add to the pan, making sure they do not jostle each other.
Brown well on both sides.
Add salt and pepper.
Sprinkle on the dry white wine.
Let evaporate.
Add the tomatoes and the consommé.
Cover the pan and simmer for about 1¾ hours.
From time to time add a little consommé to thin the sauce.
When the *ossibuchi* are tender, add the grated zest of lemon and the parsley and serve.
*Risotto* is a natural companion.
Serves six.

1 onion, chopped
3 tablespoons butter
6 veal knuckles
⅓ cup flour
Salt
Pepper
½ cup dry white wine
2 tomatoes, peeled and
   passed through sieve
1 cup beef consommé
1 teaspoon grated lemon peel
1 tablespoon chopped parsley

## 29  Risotto alla Milanese

Sauté the onions until pale gold in the mixture of butter and oil.
You will need a deep sauté pan.
Add the beef marrow.
Cook gently until it melts and becomes golden brown.
At this point, toss in the rice and stir until it becomes well coated.
After 5 minutes, add the white wine.
When the wine has been absorbed, start adding the warmed beef broth, little by little, until the rice is cooked.

½ onion, chopped
¼ cup butter
2 tablespoons olive oil
1½ tablespoons beef marrow
1 pound rice
½ cup dry white wine
5 cups beef broth
A few filaments of saffron
1 tablespoon butter
½ cup grated Parmesan cheese

Dissolve the saffron in a little hot broth and add to rice after 8 minutes.

The rice should be done in 17 to 18 minutes.

At the very last moment, stir in 1 tablespoon of butter and Parmesan cheese.

This dish will not forgive you if you keep it waiting.

Serves six.

## 30  Veal cutlets Milanese

Trim away all fat and gristle from cutlets.

Dip in beaten eggs which have been seasoned with salt and pepper.

Leave the meat in the eggs for at least 30 minutes, turning from time to time.

Coat with bread crumbs, pressing them well into meat with your hands.

Toss a generous amount of the best butter into a frying pan.

When it begins to foam, add the sage and the cutlets.

Cook over moderate heat, taking care they do not stick to pan.

When browned, they are ready to serve.

There is nothing more to it than that.

Mashed potatoes and mixed green salad make a perfect trio with the cutlets.

Serves six.

6 veal cutlets with bone
2 eggs
Bread crumbs
Salt
Pepper
Butter
1 teaspoon sage

Recipes from "Il Romanzo
della Grande Cucina"

My relationship with Maffioli, which began at the 1963 Antiques Fair, continued with a joint book called *Il Romanzo della Grande Cucina.*

The book was launched with a lunch for the press and television at the Villa Marignolle on October 7, 1965.

While the television cameras turned, Maffioli prepared one of his favorite dishes, pork William Shakespeare.

I chose to do a chicken with cucumbers because it is both simple and showy.

Nothing is worse than facing the press and television. We knew that the Italian journalists who had come to Marignolle for the launching of our book would judge us less on the printed word than on the lunch we prepared for them.

Maffioli and I couldn't have worked harder for the President of the Republic.

Since this crowd of competitive critics liked our lunch, we are fairly confident you will too.

CHICKEN LIVERS WITH GRAPES AND BLACK CHERRIES

CHICKEN WITH CUCUMBERS

ROAST SPICED PORK WILLIAM SHAKESPEARE

TIMBALE OF PEAS AND ARTICHOKES

MACEDOINE OF FRESH FRUITS

## 31 Chicken livers with grapes and black cherries

Sauté the chicken livers in the butter.
Halfway through cooking, add the grapes and the black cherries.
Sprinkle the ginger over all and serve very hot.
Serves four to six.

½ pound chicken livers
4 tablespoons butter
¼ pound grapes
¼ pound black cherries
1 teaspoon ginger

## 32 Chicken with cucumbers

There are many people who think they cannot digest cucumbers.
Probably they have never eaten them cooked. When cooked, only
the best qualities remain. They melt in your mouth. Gone is the
repetitive unpleasant aftertaste. You notice only a delightful
tartness in the sauce.

Peel ½ cucumber and slice very thin.
Toss into a saucepan with 2 tablespoons butter.
Cover and simmer for 10 minutes, by which time the cucumber
will practically have dissolved into the butter.
Add the chopped ham and cook uncovered for another 5 minutes.
Cut chicken in 8 pieces.
Flour well.
Season with salt and pepper.
Sauté chicken pieces in 2 tablespoons butter and 1 tablespoon
oil until golden brown.
Add onion and garlic.

½ medium cucumber
4 tablespoons butter
4 slices cooked ham (chopped)
1 2-pound chicken
½ cup chicken broth
½ cup white wine
1 tablespoon mixed herbs
    (thyme, sweet basil, tarragon)
2 tablespoons flour
1 tablespoon oil
1 clove garlic
1 onion
2 egg yolks
3 tablespoons cream
Salt
Pepper

Pour in white wine.

When reduced, add the broth.

Cover the pan with a lid and cook over low heat for 30 to 40 minutes.

Now remove the chicken temporarily from the casserole.

To the juices in the pan, stir in the ham and cucumber mixture, and the egg yolks which have been beaten with the cream.

Blend all the ingredients.

When the sauce thickens, return the chicken.

Heat all together and serve.

Serves four to six.


## 33   Roast spiced pork William Shakespeare

This may seem a far-fetched title, but there is a reason. Maffioli regards Shakespeare as the greatest writer in any language: He also believes that this pork recipe is the greatest in any cuisine. To indicate his admiration for it, he added the name William Shakespeare.

Make a marinade with the wine, vinegar, olive oil, celery, carrot, onion, juniper berries, rosemary, tarragon, salt, and pepper.

Rest the pork loin in the marinade for 48 hours.

Remove and brown well in the olive oil using a Dutch oven.

Pour all the marinade over the meat.

When it comes to a boil, transfer to a slow oven (300° F.).

Cook uncovered for 2 hours, turning the meat every 15 minutes.

Serve with the following sauces.

3 pounds loin of pork, with the bone left in
4 cups white wine
4 cups white wine vinegar
2 teaspoons salt
½ teaspoons pepper
2 tablespoons olive oil
1 tablespoon chopped celery
1 tablespoon chopped carrot
1 tablespoon chopped onion
1 teaspoon juniper berries
1 teaspoon rosemary
1 teaspoon tarragon

*Sauce 1*
1 grated lemon rind
Juice of 1 lemon
Worcestershire sauce
2 tablespoons raisins
1 tablespoon pine nuts
1 teaspoon cornstarch dissolved
    in 1 cup hot beef consommé
Mix all ingredients together and cook for about 5 minutes.
Serve with boiled potatoes.

*Sauce 2*
2 cups béchamel sauce
¼ cup Cognac
1 cup light cream
½ teaspoon pepper
Flame the Cognac.
Add to the béchamel with 1 cup light cream and the pepper.
Heat gently.
Serve at once with a side dish of fried apples.
Serves eight.

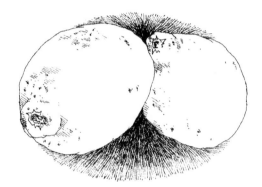

## 34  Timbale of peas and artichokes

This timbale would be good anywhere. We are chauvinistic enough
to say it is at its best in Florence, because the peas and the
artichokes from the nearby region of Empoli are reputed to be
the most tender in the world. Eat it in early spring when the
new peas are like little pellets of pale green sugar.

Shred the bacon into small pieces.
Put in a saucepan with the shelled peas, the onions, the chopped parsley, and olive oil.
Add hot water, just to cover the peas.
Season with 1 teaspoon salt and ½ teaspoon pepper.
Cover and cook over moderate heat.
For the kind of young peas we have in mind, 10 minutes will be enough.
Quarter the artichokes and remove the chokes.
(The Florentine artichoke in spring has no choke.)
Soak them in water and the juice of one lemon.
The lemon juice keeps them from darkening.
Drain and dry artichoke quarters and sauté them for 1 minute in hot olive oil.
Pour on 1 cup consommé.
Season with 1 teaspoon salt and ½ teaspoon pepper.
Cover and cook over low heat until all the consommé has been absorbed.
Make a thin béchamel sauce.
Add peas and artichokes to the sauce.
Taste for seasoning.
Pour into a soufflé dish so that the mixture reaches the top.
Prepare a pie crust.

Lay it over the top of the mixture in the soufflé dish.
Press down well on the edges with the tines of a fork.
Prick a few holes in the pastry for the steam to escape.
Brush the surface with beaten egg.
Bake in a moderate oven (350° F.) about 45 minutes when the pastry will be golden brown.
Serves eight.

3 slices salt bacon
½ pound shelled green peas
2 baby white onions
2 tablespoons chopped parsley
2 tablespoons olive oil
2 teaspoons salt
1 teaspoon pepper
8 small artichokes
Juice of 1 lemon
1 cup consommé
1 cup thin béchamel
1 basic pie crust
1 egg, beaten

Buffet at Villa Marignolle

I

# Menu VI

TRUFFLED NAPOLEON
OXTAIL PIE, BEPPE
BREAST OF CHICKEN, SIGNORA PAT
BOILED BEEF, TWICE COOKED
DRIED CODFISH WITH SPINACH
SUMMER PUDDING

## 35 Truffled Napoleon

This dish is rich as sin, and just as seductive. It is rather like a Napoleon except that the layers of puff paste, instead of being spread with a cream filling, are sandwiched with truffles and truffle paste.

We have to admit that the fresh white truffles of Piedmont which we use are quite incomparable. If you must use tinned truffles, well, you must.

Melt the butter with the flour.
Add the milk into which you have blended the well-beaten egg yolks.
Cook for about 20 minutes, stirring constantly until you have obtained a thick creamy sauce.
Add the cheese and truffle paste, the salt and pepper.
Amalgamate well.
Spread this mixture over a square sheet of baked puff pastry.
Scatter the surface with truffles, sliced razor thin.
Repeat with a second sheet of pastry and another layer of sauce and truffles.
Then the third sheet with more paste and truffles.
Top with the last layer of puff pastry.
Set into a moderate oven (350° F.) until heated through.
Cut into squares and serve hot.
Have provisions for your guests who have swooned.
Serves six.

4 layers puff pastry, pre-baked
2 tablespoons butter
2 tablespoons flour
1 quart milk
3 egg yolks
1 cup freshly grated Parmesan cheese
½ cup tinned truffle paste
½ teaspoon salt
½ teaspoon white pepper
2 fresh truffles

## 36  Oxtail pie, Beppe

Oxtail, few persons realize, has a marvelous flavor. However, we have certainly convinced hundreds of people with this oxtail pie. By using *grappa*, it becomes particularly Tuscan in flavor. (Start preparations 1 day in advance.)

Have your butcher disjoint 1 oxtail.
Brown until mahogany in butter in a Dutch oven.
Add celery, carrots, and onion and sauté, stirring constantly with wooden spoon.
Brown the flour by placing over heat in a cast iron pan, moving it gently, until it turns color.
Add the browned flour and the white wine to the mixture of sautéed vegetables and the oxtail.
When the wine has started to boil, let it simmer for a minute until half has evaporated.
Add the tomatoes, beef stock, salt and pepper, the mushrooms, the garlic clove.
Cover tightly and simmer gently for 2 hours, or until the meat falls from the bones.
We do all this the day before and refrigerate.
The fat will rise to the top. Scrape it off and discard.
Line a deep pie dish with basic pie pastry.
Fill with oxtail mixture.
Cover with pastry and brush with milk.
Slit top in several places.
Bake for 20 minutes until crust is nicely browned.
Pour the grappa through a funnel into one of the slits.
Bake for 6 minutes more.
By popular acclaim, this is one of Beppe's most fantastic dishes.
Serves six.

1 oxtail
3 tablespoons butter
½ cup chopped celery
½ cup chopped carrots
½ cup chopped onion
2 tablespoons flour
½ cup dry white wine
1 cup tomatoes, chopped coarsely
½ cup beef stock
Salt
Pepper
½ cup thinly sliced mushrooms
1 clove garlic
½ cup grappa (brandy)
Basic pie pastry for deep-dish
    2-crust pie

## 37   Breast of chicken, Signora Pat

This dish was created by Maffioli. Pat Bellini loved it.
Some men bring women flowers. Maffioli, instead, called this
chicken by the name of his hostess.
One of its greatest qualities is its adaptability. You can make it
in a great kitchen for 400 people. You can also make it in a
studio apartment for an intimate party of 4.
When you do your calculations, count on half a chicken breast per
person.

Divide chicken breasts.
Mix well the flour and the Parmesan and coat the chicken breasts.
Arrange in a low ovenproof casserole and sprinkle generously with
a mixture of the celery, rosemary, mace, and thyme.
Crumble the bouillon cube and dust the surface.
Cover with the cream.
Set in a moderate oven (350° F.) and budge from time to time
with a wooden spoon to insure even cooking.
When ready to serve, the chicken breasts should be the color of a
suntanned Scandinavian blonde.
Succulent and delicious.
Serves twelve.

6 whole chicken breasts
2 tablespoons flour
1 tablespoon grated Parmesan
   cheese
1 tablespoon finely chopped celery
1 tablespoon chopped fresh
   rosemary, or ½ tablespoon
   dried rosemary
1 teaspoon mace
1 teaspoon thyme
1 chicken bouillon cube
2 cups light cream

## 38   Dried codfish with spinach

Dried cod is one of the snubbed dishes of the world. Probably
because it was a big item in the diet of poor people. It is now
enjoying a world-wide revival and we say Hallelujah.

Wash codfish two or three times and let stand under running water all night to remove salt.
Drain and cut into squares.
Wash spinach well. Drain.
Tear into three sections per leaf.
Sauté the garlic cloves in the olive oil until golden brown.
Remove and add the tomatoes, the spinach, the consommé.
Season with pepper.
Simmer gently, giving an occasional jab, for 6 to 8 minutes.
Add the cod. Cover.
Cook from 5 to 10 minutes.
If necessary (although we doubt that it will be necessary), season with a little salt.
Serves eight.

2 pounds dried codfish
2 pounds spinach
2 cloves garlic
¼ cup olive oil
1½ cups peeled tomatoes
1 cup beef consommé
½ teaspoon pepper

## 39  Boiled beef, twice cooked

The tastiest dishes often are made from leftovers. You can frequently judge a cook by his talents with what other people might throw away.

Brown the onions slowly in the butter or oil.
Add the wine. Bring to a boil.
Add tomatoes, salt, pepper, and the beef consommé.
Cover and simmer for 30 minutes or more.
Slice the beef vertically.
(We trust you are using a juicy beef. Dry is dry.
No sauce can produce a miracle.)
Add to the tomato-onion mixture.
Cook slowly covered for another 30 minutes, tossing in a handful of chopped parsley at the end.

3 large onions, sliced thin
2 tablespoons olive oil or butter
¼ cup dry red wine
2 tablespoons peeled tomatoes
1 teaspoon salt
½ teaspoon pepper
1 cup beef consommé
1½ pounds boiled beef, already cooked
3 tablespoons chopped parsley

Serve with boiled potatoes.
The result is simple and hearty and generally brings on a smacking of the lips.
Serves six.

## 40 *Summer pudding*

This dessert came to us from England, via Pat's ancestors. It is a delightful and refreshing salute to the small fruits and berries of the lovely months of June and July.

Put all the berries in a big bowl. Sugar to taste.
You won't need much because of the natural sweetness of the fruit.
Mash into a paste.
Trim the crusts from thin slices of white bread.
Line the bottom and sides of a charlotte mold or a pudding bowl.
Pour in some of the fruit mixture.
Cover with bread slices.
Add a second abundant helping of the fruit mixture and another layer of bread until you have reached ½ inch from the top of the bowl.
Set plate on top which completely covers surface.
On this put an additional heavy weight.
The soft bread absorbs the fruit juices.
Set in refrigerator for 10 hours.
Reverse on serving platter. Unmold.
Serve with a generous dollop of whipped cream.
Enough for twelve.

1 pint strawberries, hulled
1 pint raspberries, hulled
½ pound black cherries, pitted
and quartered
½ pound red currants, stemmed
½ pound black currants, stemmed
Sugar to taste
Sliced white bread
Whipped cream

Buffet at Villa Marignolle

II

# Menu VII

CHICKEN LIVER TOASTS
ONION OMELET
LANCASHIRE HOT POT
DRIED CODFISH WITH TOMATOES
BASKET OF RAW VEGETABLES
WATERMELON SORPRESA

## 41 Chicken liver toasts

*Crostini* are a sign of hospitality in Florence. They greet you in restaurants, they welcome you in friends' homes. *Crostini* are tiny rounds of toast, spread with anchovy paste, chicken livers, cooked shellfish, cheese, or any other tidbit that happens to be in the kitchen. These little prologues to a meal are so delectable, you must watch yourself so as not to kill your appetite for what is to follow.

Clean the beef and chicken livers.
Chop the livers and onion and brown quickly in olive oil 2 or 3 minutes.
Pour in the wine and let evaporate.
Add the chopped sage and the minced garlic.
Cook for 2 minutes more and pass through a food mill.
Return to pan with 1 or 2 teaspoons of the chicken broth, the capers, the minced anchovy, salt, and pepper.
Cut the bread into thin slices.
Place in oven to toast lightly.
Moisten the toast by giving them one fast dip into the rest of the broth.
Spread with the above liver paste.
Serves ten.

6 chicken livers
½ pound beef liver
1 onion, minced
¼ cup olive oil
¼ cup dry white wine
1 tablespoon sage, chopped
1 clove garlic, minced
2 tablespoons chicken broth
1 tablespoon capers
1 anchovy, washed under
    running water
Salt
Pepper
Slices of Italian or French bread

## 42 Lancashire hot pot

I don't believe they would recognize this in Lancashire. But it does go over well with an international crowd. Since you don't have to worry about overcooking, you can keep it hot until the last bridge player has finished arguing with his partner.

Flour the chops.
Salt and pepper.
Lay in bottom of a Dutch oven.
Make a layer of thickly sliced potatoes.
Cover with layer of onions.
Continue stacking.
The top layer should be of potatoes.
Pour water to within 2 inches of the top of the casserole.
Fit on lid.
Place in hot oven until liquid starts to boil.
Lower heat and cook slowly, for 4 hours.
After 3½ hours, check seasoning.
Leave uncovered for last half-hour, so the Hot Pot browns on top.
Serves eight.

3½ pounds thick mutton chops
Flour
Salt
Pepper
3 pounds potatoes, peeled and
    sliced
4 or 5 medium onions, sliced

## 43 Onion omelet

Da Bruno is a mini-restaurant in Florence. It has only two marble-topped tables and a seating capacity of twelve. Bruno is famous because of a few specialties, among which is an extraordinary onion omelet requiring that the onions simmer in wine for 7 hours.

4 pounds onions
2 tablespoons olive oil or butter
2 cups dry red wine
8 eggs

Slice the onions.
Put in saucepan with the oil.
Fry until pale gold.
Pour in the wine.
Put lid on saucepan.
Reduce heat to lowest possible.
Simmer for 7 hours.
If liquid evaporates, add a little water.
Set the onions, which will have been reduced to a flavorful mash, in the bottom of an ovenproof pre-heated dish which you have buttered.
Beat the eggs and add on top.
Set into a moderate oven for 7 or 8 minutes.
The eggs will be cooked but still soft.
Serves four to six.

## 44   Dried codfish with tomatoes

Cod has always been one of the must dishes of Florence, because of the close vicinity of the fishing port of Livorno.

Wash the codfish well in three changes of water. Soak overnight.
Dry well and cut into 3-inch squares.
Flour the fish, dip into beaten eggs, and flour again.
Deep fry in an abundant quantity of peanut or soybean oil.
When browned on both sides, remove from pan and drain on absorbent paper.
In another pan, sauté the clove of garlic in olive oil until golden brown.

2 pounds dried codfish, soaked
    overnight in cold water
Flour
2 eggs
Soy bean or peanut oil
1 clove garlic
¼ cup olive oil
2 pounds tomatoes, peeled
1½ teaspoons pepper
Minced parsley

Remove.

Add the peeled tomatoes which have been cut into chunks.

Cook for 10 minutes.

Season with a few grinds of black pepper.

Place the cod in the tomato mixture, making sure it is covered with some of the sauce.

Cook slowly for another 10 minutes.

Serve hot with a generous sprinkling of chopped parsley over the top.

Serves six to eight.

## 45  *Watermelon surprise*

Slice off the top of a watermelon, about one fourth of the way down.

Remove the flesh down to the rind so that what you have left is a large watermelon bowl.

With a scoop, make small balls of the watermelon.

Remove as many of the seeds as possible.

Pour over the wine and liqueurs and macerate well.

Return the balls and the liquids to the watermelon shell.

Chill in a refrigerator for at least 2 hours.

Can be served as is, or further glorified with vanilla ice cream.

Serves eight to ten.

1 watermelon
1 cup dry white wine
¼ cup maraschino liqueur
2 tablespoons Cognac

Buffet at Villa Marignolle

III

# Menu VIII

MEAT SAUCE

MACARONI TIMBALE

ROAST SADDLE OF PORK MAFFIOLI

ARROSTO MORTO

VITELLO TONNATO

ZUCCHINI WITH MUSHROOMS

STUFFED TOMATOES

DATE CAKE

## 46  Meat sauce

This sauce has many uses. You can make very good dishes of baked macaroni with it. The leftover meat can be used for meatballs for the family.

Chop fine the onion, celery, carrot, parsley, basil, and salt pork or bacon.
Sauté lightly in a large pan with olive oil.
Add the pork and beef.
Slowly, slowly, slowly, cook until meat is browned.
Season with salt and pepper.
Add wine and let evaporate.
Stir in the peeled tomatoes, cut into chunks and add the tomato paste.
After a few minutes, pour on the consommé.
Cover and simmer gently for 3 hours.
Serves eight to ten.

1 large onion
1 stick celery
1 carrot
1 tablespoon parsley
1 tablespoon sweet basil
3 slices salt pork or thick bacon
½ cup olive oil
1 pound lean pork, chopped
1¼ pounds beef, chopped
2 teaspoons salt
1 teaspoon pepper
½ cup red wine
2 cups peeled tomatoes
2 tablespoons tomato paste
4 cups beef consommé

## 47  Macaroni timbale

Dressed-up pasta makes one of the most festive of party dishes. Ideal for a gala buffet is this pie.

Make a sweet pie crust.
Blend together the sifted flour, sugar, and salt.

Cut in the butter.

Stir the 3 whole eggs and the 3 egg yolks which have been well beaten.

Add the ice water little by little to obtain a dough of the right consistency.

Form into a ball.

Wrap in waxed paper and refrigerate for 30 minutes before rolling.

Prepare a béchamel sauce with 2 tablespoons flour, 2 tablespoons butter, and 2 cups of milk.

Add salt and pepper.

*Preparation of Macaroni Timbale*

Line a deep spring-form pan with the pie crust.

Save enough dough for the top.

Cook the macaroni in plenty of boiling salted water.

Optional: Scald a sweetbread in boiling water and skin it. Cut in small pieces, lightly sauté in butter, add to the above sauce, and cook for 5 minutes.

Drain the macaroni.

Mix with meat sauce and grated Parmesan.

Place a layer in the pie pan.

Cover with a layer of béchamel.

Continue until the top.

Seal with a sheet of rolled pastry.

*Pastry*

4½ cups flour
2¼ cups sugar
½ teaspoon salt
1⅓ cups butter
3 whole eggs
3 egg yolks
4 tablespoons iced water

*Béchamel sauce*

2 tablespoons butter
2 tablespoons flour
2 cups milk
1 teaspoon salt
¼ teaspoon pepper

*Macaroni Timbale*

¾ pound elbow macaroni
1 cup grated Parmesan cheese
Boiling water
3 cups meat sauce for pasta
1 egg
Optional: 1 sweetbread

Prick the surface.
Brush with beaten egg.
Set in hot oven (400° F.) for 10 minutes.
Reduce heat to moderate (350° F.) and bake for 20 minutes more.
Remove from oven and let sit cooling for 5 to 10 minutes.
Remove the sides of the spring-form pan.
Serve the timbale on a round platter.
Serves eight to ten.

## 48   Roast saddle of pork Maffioli

Ever since our friend Maffioli, the great chef of Treviso,
introduced us to this recipe, it has been one of our star
performers. It is a stalwart at a buffet for thirty people, because
you do not have to worry about a few minutes of extra cooking or
a few minutes of waiting. It is also a stylish main course for a
small luncheon or dinner. The thick well-flavored sauce that is
produced by the marinade and the slow cooking is completely
simple but gives the impression of a talented sauce cook behind
the scenes. The marinade changes pork into a party dish.
We chose this crown roast for a luncheon of ten for Piero
Bargellini, the former mayor of Florence. Since he is away most of
the time now as a senator in Rome, we wanted something sure to
please. Main table conversation was Italy's divorce law.
An American woman said she would never have been able to
marry if she felt the door was closed. "If you could not close the
door," flashed the senator, "you were not in love." Then becoming
more pragmatic, he added: "Italian men being what they are, all
of them would remarry at fifty. Italian women know us and will

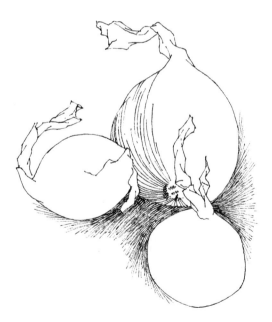

be 100 percent against a divorce law." All the guests had so much to say about love and marriage that everybody took two helpings of the roast and its delicious sauce.

The day before, place the roast in a marinade of the white wine, vinegar, sliced onions, chopped celery, rosemary, thyme, and lemon slices.
After 24 hours remove onions from the marinade and use them to line the bottom of a deep iron casserole.
Add butter and oil.
Place the meat on the onion base.
Set casserole uncovered in a moderate oven, approximately 2 hours.
Baste alternately with the marinade and milk.
When cooked, remove roast from pan.
Pass sauce through a food mill.
Pour over meat or serve separately in a sauce boat.
Serves ten to twelve.

1 4- to 5-pound loin of pork
2½ cups dry white wine
2½ cups white vinegar
3 large onions, sliced
1 stalk of celery, chopped
¼ teaspoon rosemary
¼ teaspoon thyme
1 lemon, cut in slices
2 tablespoons butter
1 tablespoon oil
Milk or cream

## 49  Arrosto morto

Rub well the surface of the veal with a little oil and butter, salt, pepper, and rosemary.
Brown well on all sides in a Dutch oven.
Add the white wine and let it evaporate.
Cover the casserole and cook over low fire for 1 hour.
Cool for a few minutes and serve sliced.
This *arrosto morto* is a fine basic for *vitello tonnato*, one of the most delightful cold summer meat dishes to be found in Italy.
Classically, a *vitello tonnato* calls for veal which has been cooked in water and white wine.
Serves six.

3 pounds boned leg of veal
Salt
Pepper
Rosemary
Butter and olive oil
1 cup dry white wine

## Vitello tonnato

As a base for *vitello tonnato*, both Beppe and I prefer veal which has been roasted either in a casserole as above, or in an oven.
When cold, cut in thin slices, spread with the following sauce, and let marinate for a day or two.

Pound together the tuna fish and well-washed anchovies.
Gradually add the olive oil so it amalgamates as if for a mayonnaise.
Squeeze in the lemon juice.
Add the capers from which you have strained the vinegar.
The sauce will be semi-thick.
Pour over the meat.
Serve in the same dish, 1 or 2 days later, garnished with lemon slices.
Serves eight to ten.

½ pound white tuna canned in oil
2 anchovy fillets
Juice of 1 to 2 lemons
Handful of capers
½ cup olive oil

## 50 Zucchini with mushrooms

Mint has a peculiar affinity for mushrooms. Around Florence grows a wild variety with a haunting scent. Locally, this wild mint is called *nepitella*.

Slice the mushrooms.
Warm a little olive oil and butter in a pan.
Put in the mushrooms, garlic, salt, pepper, and chopped mint.
Cover and steam for 10 minutes.
Add the sliced zucchini.
Cover again and cook gently for 10 minutes more.

¼ pound mushrooms
Olive oil and butter
½ teaspoon salt
½ teaspoon pepper
3 whole cloves garlic
1 teaspoon chopped mint
4 medium zucchini, sliced

## 51 Stuffed tomatoes

Nothing makes me madder than to be served in a restaurant a tomato so stuffed with rice that all the tomato flavor has been killed.
This recipe therefore is very sparing with the amount of rice used.

Slice tops from tomatoes.
Scoop out flesh from inside and mix well with rice, garlic, cheese, sage, parsley, salt, and pepper.
Bind together with 5 tablespoons olive oil.
Put back into the tomato shells.
Set in baking dish, covering the bottom with 2 tablespoons of oil.
Bake in moderate oven, 1 hour.
Serve hot or cold.
Remember: don't use boiled rice, like some people do; it comes out mushy. Me, I like it *al dente*.
Serves six.

6 large tomatoes
3 teaspoons rice
1 tablespoon parsley, finely chopped
1 clove garlic, minced
½ cup grated Parmesan cheese
1 teaspoon salt
½ teaspoon pepper
2 leaves crumbled fresh sage
7 tablespoons olive oil

## 52 Date cake

Here is another of our imports from the New World. Pat's mother brought it to us from Canada.

Cream together the butter and sugar.
Stir in the well-beaten eggs.
Add alternately, the flour which has been sifted with the baking powder and the milk.
Blend in the cinnamon, nutmeg, walnuts, and dates.
Beat all together for 2 or 3 minutes.
Pour into buttered loaf pan.
Bake in moderate oven (350° F.) for 40 minutes.

⅓ cup butter
⅓ cup brown sugar
2 eggs, well beaten
1¾ cups sifted flour
3 tablespoons baking powder
½ cup milk
½ tablespoon cinnamon
½ tablespoon nutmeg
1 cup chopped walnuts
½ pound pitted and chopped dates

Summer Lunch I

# *Menu IX*

CHEESE AND HAM CREPES
CHICKEN ALLA GIOVANNA
SPINACH ALLA MIGNON
RASPBERRY CHIFFON PIE

## 53 Cheese and ham crepes

Make a crepe batter with the flour, egg, salt, oil, and milk.
Let stand for 30 minutes in refrigerator.
Make thin crepes, 4 inches in diameter, cooking on both sides.
On each crepe, lay a small slice of ham and dot with bits of cheese.
Roll up and lay side by side in a row in a buttered baking dish.
Place in a moderate oven for 10 minutes.
Remove and cover with a béchamel sauce (1 tablespoon butter, 1 tablespoon flour, and 3 cups milk, 1 teaspoon salt, and ½ teaspoon pepper) into which you have melted the grated Parmesan and grated Gruyère.
Return to oven for another 15 minutes, until surface has been lightly browned.
Variations: Fill the crepes with a mixture of béchamel, cheese, and truffles. Another excellent filling is a mixture of fresh cottage cheese, eggs, and chopped spinach.

½ cup flour
1 egg
1 teaspoon salt
1 tablespoon oil
½ cup milk
¼ pound lean ham, sliced thin, and cut in small pieces
⅓ pound Gruyère and Fontina cheeses in small pieces

*Béchamel sauce*
1 tablespoon butter
1 tablespoon flour
3 cups milk
1 teaspoon salt
½ teaspoon pepper
½ cup grated Parmesan cheese
½ cup grated Gruyère cheese

## 54 Chicken alla Giovanna

What makes this recipe unusual is the use of grated zest of lemon. All it takes is one touch of the unexpected to transform an old dish into something new and exciting.

Brown chicken pieces in the butter, using a large sauté pan.

When browned golden on all sides, sprinkle the chicken with the flour.

Continue browning, turning the pieces about constantly.

Add the broth bit by bit, stirring with a wooden spoon.

Season with salt and pepper, and the grated lemon zest.

Lower heat.

Cover.

Simmer for 30 minutes.

Serves four.

1 2½- to 3-pound chicken, cut in 8 pieces
1 tablespoon butter
2 heaping tablespoons flour
2 cups chicken broth
1 teaspoon salt
½ teaspoon pepper
Grated zest of 1 lemon

## 55 Spinach alla Mignon

Make a béchamel sauce with the butter, the flour, the milk, and salt and pepper.

When it thickens add the spinach, and the Parmesan.

Take a buttered shallow ovenware dish and dust with bread crumbs.

Pour the spinach mixture into this dish, spreading with a spatula.

It should be about ½ inch thick.

Sprinkle over more bread crumbs and score in squares.

Dot with butter.

Bake in a hot oven (400° F.) until browned.

Serves four to six.

1 tablespoon butter
1 tablespoon flour
1 cup milk
1 teaspoon salt
½ teaspoon pepper
1 pound cooked spinach, chopped
1 cup grated Parmesan cheese
Grated bread crumbs

## 56 Raspberry chiffon pie

Drain raspberries and add water to syrup to make ⅔ cup.
Dissolve gelatin in ¾ cup hot water; add lemon juice and
raspberry syrup.
Chill till partially set.
Beat mixture till soft peaks form.
Fold in raspberries and whipped cream.
Add salt to egg whites; beat till soft peaks form.
Add sugar gradually, beating till stiff.
Fold egg whites into raspberry mixture.
Pour into cooled baked pastry shell (have edges crimped high—
filling is generous).
Chill till set.

1 10-ounce package frozen red
   raspberries, thawed
1 3-ounce package raspberry-flavored
   gelatin
¾ cup hot water
2 tablespoons lemon juice
½ cup heavy cream, whipped
Dash of salt
2 egg whites
¼ cup sugar
1 9-inch baked pastry shell

Summer Lunch II

# Menu X

STUFFED ZUCCHINI
DRUNKEN SHRIMPS WITH TOMATOES
MIXED GREEN SALAD
LEMON CHIFFON PIE
CITRUS CHIFFON PIE

## 57  Stuffed zucchini

Take a slice from the zucchini lengthwise.
Scoop out the flesh.
Mash it well with minced garlic, chopped parsley, grated Parmesan, salt, pepper.
Stir in 2 tablespoons of olive oil to bind the ingredients.
Spoon this mixture back into the hollowed zucchini.
Top with grated bread crumbs.
Set into buttered baking dish.
Cover bottom of dish with 1 cup consommé.
Cook in moderate oven about 1 hour.
Serves six.

6 large zucchini
1 clove garlic, minced
2 tablespoons chopped parsley
1 teaspoon salt
½ teaspoon pepper
2 tablespoons olive oil
1 cup grated Parmesan cheese
Grated bread crumbs
1 cup consommé

## 58  Drunken shrimps with tomatoes

Don't be cheap with your Cognac. Unless you use a good quality, you will have short-changed this dish. That would be very poor economy indeed.

Pour ⅓ cup olive oil into a large pan.
Sauté lightly the chopped onion, celery, carrot, parsley, and sweet basil.
Add the peeled tomatoes which have been cut in chunks.
Season with salt, pepper, and bay leaf.
Cook slowly uncovered for 45 minutes.

Strain through a food mill and set aside.
Wash and dry well the shrimps.
Flour them thoroughly.
Dip in beaten egg yolks.
Heat butter rapidly.
Fry a few at a time in the foaming butter.
As soon as the shrimps take on a gold color, remove, and drain on paper towels.
If you need more butter, don't hesitate.
When all are cooked, return to pan.
Souse them with Cognac and ignite.
Add the tomato sauce.
Simmer gently for 5 minutes taking care the shrimps do not stick to bottom of pan.
Serve hot with fluffy, boiled rice.
Serves eight to ten.

⅓ cup olive oil
1 medium onion, chopped
1 stalk celery
1 carrot
1 tablespoon parsley
4 leaves sweet basil
4 cups peeled tomatoes
1½ teaspoons salt
½ teaspoon pepper
1 bay leaf
2 pounds shrimp, shelled
Flour
2 eggs
½ pound butter
2 cups Cognac

## 59  Lemon chiffon pie

We are so used to thinking in terms of emigration from Europe that we sometimes forget that the Atlantic Ocean is a two-way thoroughfare. One of the favorite desserts in Beppe's house for all his Italian friends is an American lemon chiffon pie. His guests literally cry over it. Beppe is mad about the clean fresh taste of lemons. I like this pie even better in a version called citrus chiffon pie, which uses the juice of both lemons and oranges. Either way, it has won as many friends for America as blue jeans and cowboy movies.

Thoroughly mix gelatin, ½ cup sugar, and salt in saucepan.
Beat together egg yolks, lemon juice and water; stir into gelatin mixture.
Cook and stir over medium heat just till mixture comes to a boil.
Remove from heat; stir in lemon peel.
Chill, stirring occasionally, till mixture is partially set.
Beat egg whites till soft peaks form.
Gradually add ½ cup sugar, beating to stiff peaks; fold in gelatin mixture.
Pile in cooled baked pastry shell.
Chill until firm.
Spread with sweetened whipped cream before serving.
Or cream may be folded into filling with egg whites.

1 envelope (1 tablespoon) unflavored gelatin
½ cup sugar
½ teaspoon salt
4 egg yolks
⅓ cup lemon juice
⅔ cup water
1 teaspoon grated lemon peel
4 egg whites
½ cup sugar
1 9-inch baked pastry shell
½ cup heavy cream, whipped

## 60 Citrus chiffon pie

Thoroughly mix gelatin, ½ cup sugar, and salt in saucepan.
Beat together egg yolks, fruit juices, and water.
Stir into gelatin mixture.
Cook and stir over medium heat just till mixture comes to a boil.
Remove from heat; stir in peels.
Chill, stirring occasionally, till mixture mounds slightly when dropped from a spoon.
Beat egg whites till soft peaks form.
Gradually add ⅓ cup sugar, beating to stiff peaks; fold in gelatin mixture.
Pile into cooled baked pastry shell.
Chill till firm.
Trim with whipped cream and thin quartered orange slices.

1 envelope (1 tablespoon) unflavored gelatin
½ cup sugar
Dash of salt
4 egg yolks
½ cup lemon juice
½ cup orange juice
¼ cup water
½ teaspoon grated lemon peel
½ teaspoon grated orange peel
4 egg whites
⅓ cup sugar
1 9-inch baked pastry shell

Italian Lunch
for Friends from Abroad

Florence gets more than 1,000,000 visitors every year. Not bad for a city whose population is 400,000. This is why we have a never-ending kaleidoscope of guests.

When most of our guests are from abroad, we concentrate on Florentine specialties, the kind rarely found in restaurants because of their last-minute preparations. When the guests are from Roma, Milano, Treviso, we like to introduce them to a few foreign specialties. Most of our menus are for a minimum of twelve persons. To simplify them for people who are not so lucky to live in a city like Florence, we have reduced the proportions.

RICOTTA DUMPLINGS

VEAL COOKED IN MILK

FRESH LETTUCE SALAD WITH
DRESSING

ASSORTED CHEESES

FRUIT OF THE SEASON

ZUCCOTTO

## 61  Ricotta dumplings

I first tasted these delectable dumplings in Beppe's town house in Florence. Probably more than anything else, they seduced me into preparing this book with him. Beppe has only one complaint about them. Guests beg so hard for a taste that he is forced to make them too often.

2 pounds spinach
1 pound ricotta cheese
2 cups grated Parmesan cheese
3 eggs, beaten
1 teaspoon pepper
¼ teaspoon grated nutmeg
Flour

Wash spinach well.
Drain.
Cook in a deep saucepan with no water.
(Enough water clings to the leaves.)
When cooked, drain again.
Squeeze the spinach with your hands to extract as much liquid as possible.
Chop fine.
Mix with ricotta cheese, 1 cup of grated Parmesan, the beaten eggs, salt, pepper, and nutmeg.
When all ingredients are well combined, shape into the form of small eggs, using a tablespoon.
Roll "eggs" in flour.
Drop several dumplings at a time into a large saucepan of boiling water.
They will rise to the top in about 1 minute.
Remove with a slotted spoon and neatly align them in a shallow buttered ovenware dish.
Pour on melted butter and grated Parmesan.

Guard in slow heated oven as you go on boiling the rest of the dumplings.
Continue to pour on more melted butter and Parmesan as you add the dumplings to the dish.
Serve immediately.
Once on the table, they disappear in no time at all.
Serves six to eight.

## 62  Veal cooked in milk

Around Florence, veal is not only milk fed but often cooked in milk as well. The result is meat that literally melts in your mouth.

Brown the meat well in butter in a Dutch oven.
Add the onions and continue cooking until they are pale gold.
Pour in 1 cup of scalded milk, adding the second cup later on.
Cover.
Cook slowly for about 3 hours.
The sauce will be like a creamy gravy.
(If any lumps have formed, strain them out.)
Pour over the meat or serve apart in a sauce boat.
This recipe could serve eight.

3 pounds rolled boneless leg of veal
¼ pound butter
2 sliced fine onions
2 cups hot milk

## 63  Zuccotto

A *zucca* is a pumpkin, a gourd, or a round head. The *zuccotto*, one of the richest and most famous desserts in Florence, gets its name because of its round melon shape.

Line a deep large bowl or mold with strips of spongecake or lady fingers moistened with maraschino.

Whip 2 cups of heavy cream.

Sweeten with ½ cup sugar and flavor with vanilla.

Fold in ½ cup candied fruit.

Spoon the mixture into the cake-lined mold.

This makes the first layer of filling.

Melt 3 ounces semi-sweet chocolate with ¾ cup water in a double boiler.

Stir in ½ tablespoon Cognac.

Cool.

Whip 2 cups of heavy cream until stiff.

Fold in the cold chocolate sauce.

Spoon over the candied fruit filling to make a second layer.

Whip another 2 cups heavy cream with ½ cup of sugar until stiff.

Fold in ¾ cup mashed strawberries.

Spoon over the chocolate filling to make a third layer.

Freeze the dessert until it is firm.

To serve, unmold on a chilled platter, and cut into wedges.

Serves eight.

Spongecake (or lady fingers)
Maraschino liqueur
6 cups heavy whipping cream
1 cup sugar
¼ teaspoon vanilla
1 cup candied fruit
3 ounces semi-sweet chocolate
½ tablespoon Cognac
¾ cup mashed strawberries

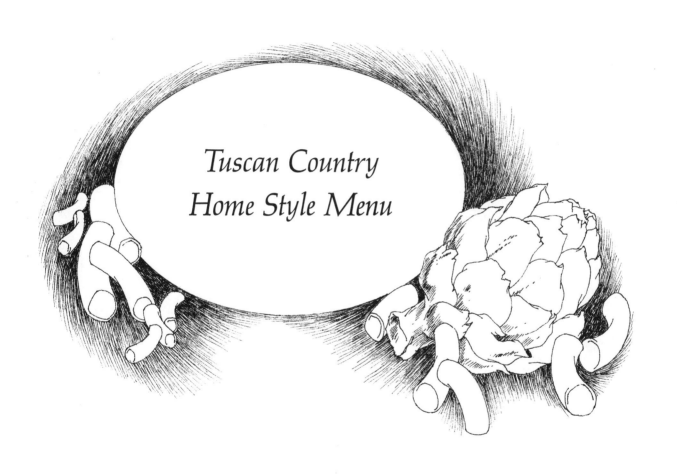

Tuscan Country
Home Style Menu

This menu is a country-style lunch as you might find it in a Tuscan home. Its simplicity is rather typical. Main dish is *stracotto*, a tasty beef stew for which Florentines will give any price. It is somewhat different from the *stracotto* of all other regions.

The dessert follows that excellent local custom of eating cheese with sweet, juicy pears. An old Tuscan saying goes: "Don't let the peasants know how good is the pear with the cheese." Apparently, the aristocratic town dwellers felt that if the peasants knew what a delicacy they had at hand, they would keep the best cheese and pears for themselves instead of sending them to market.

ANTIPASTO: Use all your artistry to prepare an attractive platter. In Florence, it would include prosciutto, salami, *finocchiona* (a local salami flavored with fennel seeds), anchovies. Anything goes: Olives, hard-boiled egg, green peppers cut in strips, radishes, hearts of celery, carrot sticks.

ANTIPASTO

PENNE STRASCICATE (PASTA WITH MEAT SAUCE)

STRACOTTO ALLA FIORENTINA — BEEF STEW

ARTICHOKES MASQUERADING AS MUSHROOMS

PECORINO CHEESE WITH PEARS

## 64 Stracotto alla Fiorentina – beef stew

Brown the beef slowly and well in the oil and butter in a Dutch oven.
Put in the diced salt pork and the pork chop at the same time.
Finely chop onions, carrots, and celery.
Add to the Dutch oven.
Stir until they take on a pale brown color.
Pour in the red wine.
Let evaporate.
Add the tomato paste, salt, and pepper, and the consommé. Cover with a tight-fitting lid and simmer for 2½ hours.
Remove the beef and the pork chop.
Cover to keep warm.
Cut the beef in slices after 5 minutes.
(Give the pork chop to the dog as a special treat.
It was only used to flavor the *stracotto*.)
Divide your sauce in two parts. Half goes over the meat.
The other half is reserved for the pasta.
Serves eight.

3 to 4 pounds beef (rump or bottom round) well marbled
½ cup butter and olive oil
¼ pound salt pork, diced
1 pork chop
½ cup chopped onions
½ cup chopped carrots
½ cup chopped celery
½ cup red wine (preferably Chianti)
1 tablespoon tomato paste
2 teaspoons salt
1 teaspoon pepper
2 cups beef consommé

## 65 Penne strascicate (pasta with meat sauce)

Meanwhile have ready your *penne*, cooked and drained.
Warm an ovenware serving dish.
Cover the bottom with 2 tablespoons melted butter.

Add the cooked pasta and let heat up for a few seconds.
Pour on the meat sauce and 1 cup of grated Parmesan.
Mix and stir until all the pasta is well coated.
Serve in the same dish.
Serves six.

1 pound *penne* (or other short,
    thick pasta in tube form)
2 tablespoons butter
Meat sauce (recipe 46)
1 cup grated Parmesan cheese

## 66  *Artichokes masquerading as mushrooms*

There is an old Russian proverb, "If you think you are a mushroom, jump into the basket." This proverb must have spread to Tuscany, because our delicious artichokes sometime ask to be treated as if they were mushrooms.

Peel off hard outer leaves of artichokes.
Slice lengthwise in quarters.
Remove choke.
Soak in cold water with lemon slices to keep artichokes from darkening.
Sauté the garlic with olive oil.
When pale gold, discard garlic.
Drain the artichoke quarters and dry.
Put in the pan to sauté over low heat.
After 2 minutes, pour in the hot consommé.
Season with salt and pepper.
Cook slowly for 30 minutes, or until tender when pierced with a fork.
Sprinkle with chopped parsley.
Serves six.

6 medium artichokes
2 slices lemon
1 clove garlic
½ cup olive oil
1 cup beef consommé
½ teaspoon salt (optional)
½ teaspoon pepper
Handful of chopped parsley

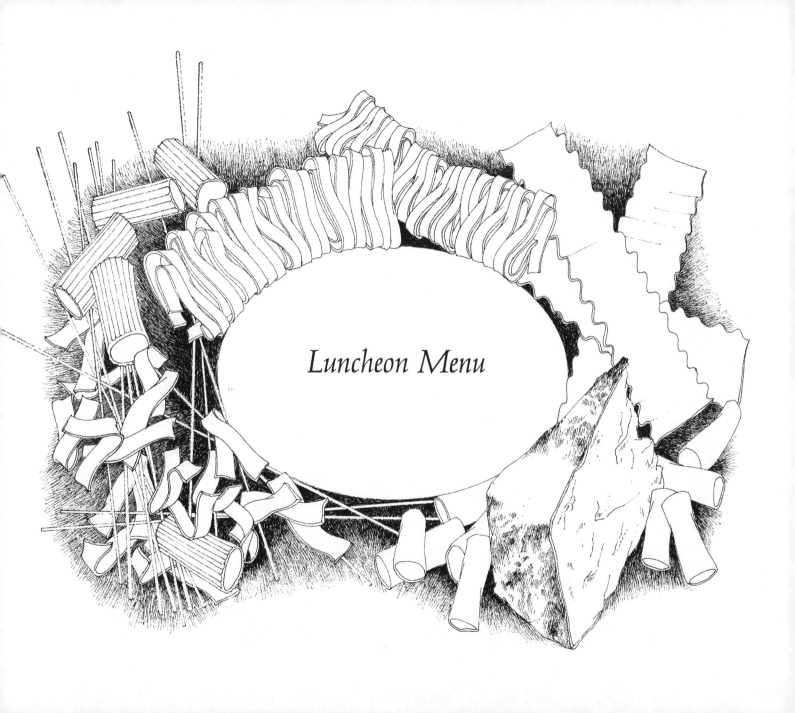

Luncheon Menu

LASAGNE

LASAGNE WITH FOUR CHEESES

MIXED BOILED MEATS WITH GREEN
    SAUCE

CHINESE CHEWS

## 67 Lasagne

Making pasta at home is less complicated than you might think, although, it does require patience and time. The more expert you become, the less time you will need. The results, however, justify your efforts.

4 cups flour
5 eggs, well beaten
1 teaspoon salt
Water

Heap flour in a mound on a board.
Make a well in center. Pour in eggs and salt.
Add about 2 tablespoons of water.
Work the liquids into the flour with your fingers.
Form the pasta into a soft ball.
Wipe away from the board any of the egg and flour that have not been absorbed.
Sprinkle the ball of pasta with a light coat of flour.
Knead the dough for 10 to 15 minutes with heel of your hand until light and elastic.
Divide the dough into 3 or 4 pieces.
With a long wooden rolling pin, roll out each piece of dough into very thin sheets.
Flour and turn from time to time.
It should become as thin as a semi-transparent cloth.
Let it rest for 30 minutes.
It's not a bad idea to hang the sheets of dough over a clothesline in the kitchen to dry.
For the *lasagne*, cut each sheet of dough into strips two inches wide.
The length is determined by the length of the baking dish you are going to use.

## 68   Lasagne with four cheeses

*Lasagne* with one cheese is good. With two cheeses, it is better.
With three it is almost perfect. With four, it is pure bliss.
For this kind of heaven, the *lasagne* must be homemade.

Cook the sheets of *lasagne* in a large pot of furiously boiling
salted water.
The addition of 1 tablespoon olive oil to the water will keep
the pasta from sticking.
When *al dente*, cooked to a firm stage, remove carefully with
forceps.
Lay to drain on paper towels.

*Sauce*

While the *lasagne* is cooking start preparing the sauce.
Melt 2 tablespoons butter.
Add 2 tablespoons of flour.
Stir in gradually 4 cups of milk, obtaining a smooth white sauce.
Add the Gruyère, the Parmesan, the pecorino and the mozzarella,
salt and pepper.
Blend in thoroughly.
Cover the bottom of a buttered ovenware dish with sheets of
*lasagne.*
Pour over some of the sauce.
Repeat until all the *lasagne* and all the sauce has been used.
There should be at least 4 layers.
Bake in a moderate oven (350° F.) for 45 minutes until golden
brown on top.
Serves six.

1 pound *lasagne*
2 tablespoons flour
2 tablespoons butter
4 cups milk
1½ cups grated Gruyère cheese
1½ cups grated Parmesan cheese
1½ cups grated pecorino cheese
1½ cups diced mozzarella cheese
1½ teaspoons salt
1 teaspoon white pepper

## 69 Green sauce for mixed boiled meats

*Bollito misto* (mixed boiled meats) has Italians up and down the peninsula smacking their lips. With it, they eat a fabulous green sauce.

Take away the boiled meats. I, personally, hate them, but would willingly eat a bowl of the sauce with a spoon. Anyway, the green sauce is a superb accompaniment to any cold meat. Boil the meat and serve with the following sauce.

Soak the crumbled bread in the vinegar.
Squeeze dry.
Mix together the parsley, capers, gherkins, washed anchovy fillet, hard-boiled egg, and garlic, all of which have been chopped fine.
Mix in the bread crumbs.
Add enough olive oil to cover, and a drop of lemon juice.
There should be plenty of parsley to give a good green color.
The sauce will be rather thick.
Beppe's personal touch to a *salsa verde* is to add a teaspoon of sugar and a tablespoon of Cognac.
This makes the sauce a kind of sweet-and-sour.

½ cup crumbled stale bread
1 tablespoon vinegar
½ cup chopped parsley
1 tablespoon chopped capers
2 gherkins, chopped
1 anchovy fillet, chopped
1 hard-boiled egg, well chopped
1 clove garlic, minced
2 tablespoons olive oil
Lemon juice
1 teaspoon sugar
1 tablespoon Cognac

## 70 Chinese chews

We have no idea why these chewy cakes are attributed to the Chinese. Our only guess, and a farfetched one, is that someone had them in a British house in Hong Kong. They are delicious, even if unknown in origin.

Butter and flour a shallow oblong baking pan.
Mix dry ingredients.
Add the chopped dates and nuts.
Stir in the well-beaten eggs.
Spread the mixture into the baking pan.
Bake in moderate oven (350° F.) 30 minutes.
Cut in 2-inch squares.
While still warm, press in granulated sugar on top and bottom.

1 cup sugar
¾ cup flour
1 teaspoon baking powder
1 teaspoon cinnamon
¼ teaspoon ground cloves
Pinch of salt
1 cup chopped walnuts
1 cup chopped dates
2 eggs
Granulated sugar

Almost Formal Dinner

# Menu XIV

LIVER PÂTÉ

ONION SOUP

ASPARAGUS WITH CHEESE

DUCK IN ORANGE SAUCE

MOUSSE AU CHOCOLAT

## 71  Liver pâté

Sauté the pieces of liver in the butter with chopped onion for 5 minutes.
Then add Cognac and let evaporate.
Add the sage and garlic.
Pass through food mill.
Make a béchamel sauce.
Season with salt and pepper.
Combine the liver mixture with the béchamel.
Make an aspic by dissolving unflavored gelatin in ¼ cup cold water.
Heat 1½ cups consommé.
Stir in the dissolved gelatin until melted.
Pour 1 inch into bottom of a rectangular mold.
Cool until firm in the refrigerator.
Pack the liver mixture into mold.
Seal the top with another inch coating of aspic.
Keep in refrigerator until ready to use.
Unmold by setting into a bowl of hot water for 1 minute.
Turn out on serving dish.
Garnish with parsley and tomato wedges.
Serves ten to twelve.

1 pound calf's liver, cut in
  small pieces
1 pound chicken livers chopped fine
3 tablespoons butter
1 onion chopped fine
½ cup Cognac
2 tablespoons chopped sage
2 cloves garlic, minced
Salt
Pepper

*Béchamel sauce*
2 tablespoons butter
2 tablespoons flour
2 cups milk
Salt
Pepper

*Aspic*
1½ cups chicken broth
½ envelope unflavored gelatin

## 72 Asparagus with cheese

The town of Pescia, near Montecatini, is the asparagus capital of Italy. Here the stalks grow taller and fatter than in any other place I know.

A restaurateur of Pescia completely changed my techniques for boiling asparagus. Until then, I had always boiled them upright with the tips out of the water. In fact, I even had made a special pot for this purpose.

Cecco's advice follows. Since we took it, we have never tasted more tender asparagus, always cooked to just the right degree.

½ pound asparagus per person
2 tablespoons melted butter per pound
2 tablespoons freshly grated Parmesan cheese per pound
Salt

Wash asparagus thoroughly, taking pains to remove sandy grit lurking in the tips.

Cut off the tough ends of the stalks.

Scrape or peel each stalk up from the bottom for 2 or 3 inches. Tie stalks in bunches.

Have plenty of salted water boiling furiously in a container tall enough to cover entire stalk.

Set in pot vertically, but with the heads pointing down.

The natural reaction is fear that the tips will be bruised.

This does not happen.

Cook for 7 to 8 minutes, depending on the thickness of the stalk.

This topsy-turvy method insures even cooking of the entire length of the asparagus.

Drain the asparagus and arrange in a well-buttered ovenproof dish.

Sprinkle the green part with freshly grated Parmesan.

Pour over the melted butter.

Place under a broiler flame until the cheese melts and the top is brown and bubbly.

## 73　Duck in orange sauce

Italians have been preparing duck with orange practically since the beginning of our recorded history.

Wash and dry the duck well.
Rub with coarse salt.
Set in hot oven for 15 minutes.
Lower heat to moderate.
Count 20 minutes per pound.
When cooked, cut in 8 portions, and arrange in ovenware dish.
Skim off the fat that has collected in the roasting pan.
Stir in the cornstarch.
Place pan over low heat.
Add the broth, stirring constantly with a wooden spoon to scrape up any bits of meat that have collected at the bottom.
Pour in the orange and lemon juice.
Boil the sugar and vinegar and add to sauce.
When the sauce has become slightly caramelized, pour over the duck which is waiting in the ovenproof dish.
Set the duck and sauce back in a slow oven to reheat.
Ignite the Cognac and pour over.
Serves four.

1 5- to 6-pound duck
1 tablespoon coarse salt
1 teaspoon pepper
1 cup white wine
1 tablespoon cornstarch
1 cup chicken broth
Juice of 5 oranges
Juice of 1 lemon
3 tablespoons sugar
¼ cup vinegar
¼ cup Cognac

## 74　Chocolate mousse

Melt the squares of chocolate and the butter with the water in the top of a double boiler.
Remove from stove.
Cool.

Beat the egg yolks and stir into the chocolate mixture.
Beat the 6 egg whites stiff, incorporating the sugar.
Fold into the chocolate mixture.
Put in a crock and chill in the refrigerator.
If you prefer it not so "chocolaty," mix with whipped cream which lightens the color and produces a more delicate flavor.
Serves six.

10 squares semi-sweet baking
   chocolate
1 tablespoon butter
4 tablespoons water
4 eggs plus 2 egg whites
3 tablespoons sugar

Dinner at Nine for Six

# Menu XV

MANGO CANAPÉS

RICE MOLD, MARILENA

FILLETS OF SOLE

PHEASANT ALLA CREMA

TUSCAN APPLE TART

## 75  Mango canapés

At cocktail parties all over the world, there tends to be a monotony to the canapés and accompaniments to drinks. We took a little inspiration from India to jazz up our cocktail party trays in Florence.

Slice thinly a loaf of white sandwich bread.
Make small rounds with a glass or a cookie cutter.
Sauté in butter on both sides, until pale gold.
Drain on paper towels.
Beat the eggs in a bowl.
Add cream, salt, and pepper.
Cook with the butter in the top of a double boiler.
Stir until you have a creamy mixture.
Remove from fire.
Spoon onto the toasted bread rounds.
Garnish each round with a small piece of mango from the mango chutney.
Serve very hot.
Serves ten to twelve.

Loaf of white sandwich bread
Butter
Eggs
Cream
Salt
Pepper
Small piece of butter
Mango chutney

## 76  Rice mold Marilena

Boil the rice, using the recipe for *risotto*.
Mix with ¼ pound butter.
Stir in 1 cup of mixed grated Parmesan and Gruyère.

Place half of this mixture in a buttered mold.
Top with a layer of ham and mozzarella.
Cover with the rest of the rice.
Bake in moderate oven for 20 minutes.
Make a béchamel with the 1½ tablespoons butter, the flour, and the milk.
Stir in ½ cup mixed Parmesan and Gruyère.
Unmold the rice on a serving platter.
Nap with the cheese-flavored béchamel.
Serve the rest in a sauce boat.
Serves six.

½ pound rice
¼ pound butter
1½ cup grated Parmesan and Gruyère cheeses
⅓ cup chopped boiled ham
¼ pound mozzarella cheese, diced
1½ tablespoons butter
1½ tablespoons flour
2 cups milk

## 77   Fillets of sole

Sprinkle salt and pepper into the flour.
Flour well the fillets of sole.
Sauté the chopped onion in the butter and oil until soft.
Add the fillets of sole, and sauté on each side until golden brown.
Pour on the white wine and let evaporate.
Remove the fish fillets and arrange them in an ovenware dish.
Meanwhile have minced together the walnuts, hard-boiled eggs, parsley and the grated zest of lemon.
Sprinkle a little of this mixture on top of each fillet.
Dust with the grated Gruyère.
Pour over the liquid from the sauté pan.
Brown in oven.
Serve very hot.
Serves six.

1 teaspoon salt
¼ teaspoon pepper
3 tablespoons flour
12 fillets of sole
1 onion, finely chopped
1 tablespoon butter
1 tablespoon olive oil
½ cup dry white wine
½ cup shelled walnuts
2 hard-boiled eggs
Parsley
Zest of 1 lemon, grated
½ cup grated Gruyère cheese

## 78 Pheasant alla crema

Rub into the pheasant, the mixture of chopped garlic, chopped rosemary, and chopped sage.
Bard the breast with the slices of salt pork.
Bake in a covered roasting pan in a moderate oven for about 1 hour.
Remove the lid to allow the bird to brown for 30 minutes.
Take out of the oven, but keep in warm place, removing the slices of pork.
Strain the sauce into a saucepan.
Add mustard, Worcestershire sauce, and cream.
Ignite the Cognac and pour into the pan.
Heat all together for 3 or 4 minutes.
If the sauce seems too liquid, thicken with the cornstarch which has been dissolved in a tablespoon of water.
Cut the pheasant into 8 pieces.
Pour over the sauce and reheat in slow oven for 5 minutes.
Serves four.

1 2-pound dressed pheasant
1 clove garlic, minced
1 teaspoon rosemary
1 teaspoon sage
¼ pound salt pork, sliced
1 teaspoon mustard
1 tablespoon Worcestershire sauce
1 cup light cream
2 tablespoons Cognac
1 teaspoon cornstarch (optional)

## 79 Tuscan apple tart

Peel and slice the apples thinly.
Steep for several hours in the whisky to which you have added 3 tablespoons of sugar.
Cream the ½ cup sugar and butter.
Add the eggs and sift in the flour and salt.
Make a pastry with light hands.
Set the ball of dough in the refrigerator for 30 minutes.
Butter and flour a pie plate and line with the pastry dough.

5 medium apples
1 small glass of whisky
3 tablespoons sugar
½ cup sugar
¼ pound butter
3 eggs
2 cups flour
½ teaspoon salt

Drain the apples (saving the juice) and fill the pie dish.
Make a lattice-work top with strips of pastry.
Brush the surface with beaten egg.
Bake in moderate oven until pastry is golden brown.
Pour the whisky and juice over the apples.
Serves six.

Dinner at the Fair

## Menu XVI

BROCCOLI SOUFFLÉ

SCALOPPE ALLA ITALIAN PAVILLON

ONION AND TOMATO CASSEROLE

MAPLE MOUSSE

## 80 Broccoli soufflé

The pale green of the broccoli gives an alluring note to this soufflé.

Melt the butter, add flour and cook 2 minutes, stirring all the time.
Pour in the milk and stir till thickened.
Add Parmesan, salt and pepper, and put aside.
Beat egg yolks and add to the mixture one at a time.
Incorporate the broccoli purée.
Beat egg whites until stiff and fold into cooled mixture.
Pour into buttered soufflé dish and bake in a moderate oven (350° F.) about 45 minutes.
*Note:* Any puréed vegetable can be substituted for the broccoli.
Serves six.

3 tablespoons butter
3 tablespoons flour
1 cup milk
1 cup grated Parmesan cheese
Salt
Pepper
3 egg yolks
1 cup cooked broccoli passed
   through food mill
4 egg whites

## 81 Scaloppe all'Italian pavillon

The World's Fair of 1939 brought some of Europe's best chefs to New York. The outbreak of World War II stranded a lot of them there. The majority of the staffs of the French and Italian pavilions stayed on to establish some of the finest restaurants in New York.
A waiter from the Italian Pavilion became a part-time cook for me, before I joined the American Army. From him I learned these scallops.

Cut open each veal scallop and spread like the two leaves of a book.
Pound flat.
Trim the fat from the prosciutto and place a slice on half of each veal scallop.
Top with a slice of cheese.
Season with salt and pepper.
Fold the meat over and press the edges well together, thus closing the book.
Dip in the beaten eggs and then in bread crumbs.
Pat with your hands so that the bread crumbs adhere well to the scallops.
Heat the butter.
Fry the scallops on each side.
Pour in the Cognac and ignite.
Serve immediately.
Serves six.

1½ pounds milk-fed veal scallops, cut fairly thick
¼ pound prosciutto, cut into thin slices
⅓ pound sliced Gruyère or Parmesan cheese
Salt
Pepper
2 eggs
Bread crumbs
1⅓ cups butter
4 tablespoons Cognac

## 82   Onion and tomato casserole

Place in ovenproof casserole, the tomatoes, onion, bread, salt, pepper, and sage.
Dot with butter.
Bake in hot oven (400° F.) for about 45 minutes.
This is a convenient vegetable dish for a day you are making a roast since both can be cooked in the oven at the same time.
Serves six to eight.

2 cups peeled chopped tomatoes or 1 can peeled Italian tomatoes
½ cup chopped onion
2½ cups stale bread broken in pieces
1 teaspoon salt
½ teaspoon pepper
1 teaspoon chopped sage
3 tablespoons butter

## 83 Maple mousse

Mix the maple syrup with beaten egg yolks.
Cook on a slow fire until boiling point.
Let cool.
Then beat until light.
Add maple flavoring.
Whip the egg whites until firm, and the cream until stiff.
Add both to maple mixture.
Sprinkle the chopped walnuts and cherries over the bottom of
a mold or soufflé dish.
Pour in mousse mixture.
Place in freezing compartment of refrigerator.
Unmold, by setting in a bowl of hot water for a second.
Turn out at once and serve.
If this is too much for you, present the mousse in the soufflé
dish.
Serves six.

1 cup maple syrup
4 eggs, separated
1 pint heavy cream
1 teaspoon maple flavoring
½ cup mixed green and red
　　candied cherries
Chopped walnuts

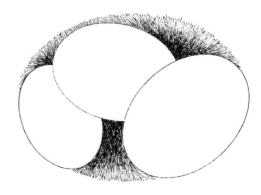

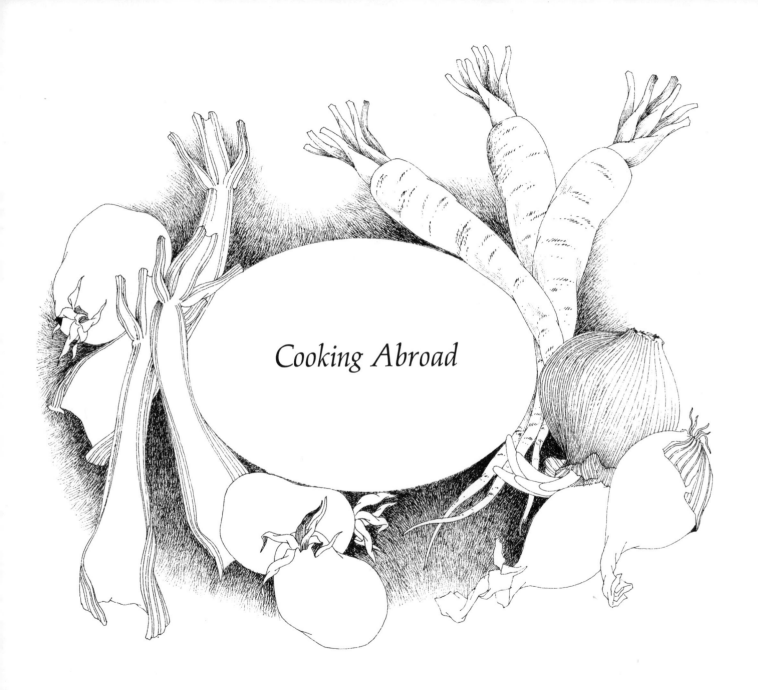

Cooking Abroad

When I was twenty-two, my father sent me to Paris. I was
supposed to go to the Sorbonne to study art history. I was also
supposed to polish up my French. In addition, I was supposed to
attend sales and report on the art world to my father.

Mostly I learned about Paris by night. I had a friend from Naples,
Baron Davella, who was working as a representative of Perrier-Jouet
champagne. He easily convinced me to accompany him every
night to check up on sales in all the night clubs like Casanova
and Chez Florence. He was such a conscientious worker that
somehow we never went home until four in the morning and
then with a crowd of people we had met. By that time everybody
was very hungry.

In Paris I became an expert in making spaghetti with tomato
sauce. It was cheap, it was filling, and it was quick to prepare.
I must say that since my student days, this recipe never failed
to help me make friends.

Two years later when I went to New York to represent my father,
this same spaghetti made me welcome at every party. Even today,
we find it a fantastic dish when we are home alone.

SPAGHETTI AND TOMATO SAUCE

RIGATONI WITH MEAT SAUCE

VEAL SCALLOPINE AL MARSALA

ARTICHOKE OMELET

VEAL BIRDS

FONDUE PIEDMONT STYLE

LOBSTER BILL

ONION SOUP, BEPPE STYLE

PEPERONATA CONTADINA

CONSOMMÉ WITH SHERRY

CHICKEN BAKED IN MILK

SCALLOPED POTATOES

BROCCOLI

PRUNE SOUFFLÉ

RISOTTO WITH SHELLFISH

## 84 Spaghetti and tomato sauce

Gently heat butter and olive oil in a large frying pan, and add I clove of garlic until brown.

Remove garlic and in the same pan sauté the onion until golden.

Drain the juice from the tomatoes and toss only the pulp into pan.

Add the sage.

Stir with a fork until well heated but not cooked.

Add the salt, freshly ground pepper, and the sugar.

Meanwhile, boil the spaghetti in a large pot of boiling water.

Stop the cooking the moment the spaghetti begins to curl.

The secret of successful spaghetti is plenty of water that has been salted until it is salty to the taste.

The water should be boiling furiously before you drop in the pasta.

Immediately separate the strands with a fork.

As soon as they are *al dente*, add a little cold water to stop the cooking.

Drain.

Then quickly, back with them into the big empty pot which is still warm.

Pour over the heated tomato mixture, a large dose of grated Parmesan cheese.

Stir vigorously and serve.

Serves four.

1 tablespoon butter
2 tablespoons olive oil
1 clove garlic
1 large red onion, coarsely chopped
1 1-pound can peeled Italian tomatoes (only the pulp)
1 teaspoon dried sage or 2 leaves fresh sage
1 teaspoon salt
½ teaspoon freshly ground pepper
½ teaspoon sugar
1 pound spaghetti
Grated Parmesan cheese

## 85 Rigatoni with meat sauce

Back in the days when I was living mainly on pasta, we used to make a festive evening on *rigatoni* with the following meat sauce. *Rigatoni* is a thick short noodle which should be cooked the same way as spaghetti.

You begin with a *soffritto* or a *battuto*, which is nothing more than 1 onion, 1 carrot, 1 clove of garlic, some celery leaves, and some parsley, all finely chopped and browned in oil or butter in a Dutch oven with finely diced bacon.
Add the pork and the beef, cut into large chunks, to the pan and brown well.
Pour on red wine and let alcohol evaporate.
Add the pulp of the canned tomatoes and tomato paste.
After 2 minutes, stir in one can of beef broth.
Since you need enough liquid to cover all the ingredients, you may have to add a little water.
Place a lid on the Dutch oven.
Simmer for 3 hours.
Remove the meat, serve the sauce on cooked *rigatoni*.
The meat was the basis of a meal the next day.
We were very budget minded.
Serves four.

1 pound *rigatoni*
1 onion
1 carrot
1 clove garlic
Celery leaves
Parsley
Olive oil
Butter
Bacon
½ pound pork loin
1 pound beef stew meat
½ cup red wine
1 can Italian tomatoes
2 tablespoons tomato paste
1 can beef broth

## 86 Veal scallopine al Marsala

To make a fast impression on the young ladies who occasionally came to my Paris student apartment for dinner, I taught myself to become an expert in preparing veal scallopine.

Veal in France is of excellent quality. Furthermore, many veal dishes are rapid to make, so I did not have to spend too much time in the kitchen, for I must admit that my interests were mainly elsewhere.

A good veal scallopine is just a matter of technique.
Soak the scallopine in beaten egg for at least 1 hour.
Dredge with flour.
Pound the flour into the meat with your hand so that it penetrates all the pores and covers the meat evenly.
Season with salt and pepper.
Melt butter (use enough butter to cover the bottom of the pan).
Brown the meat, taking pains not to burn it.
This requires careful watching.
Curiously enough, even many professional cooks do not know how to sauté without burning.
After browning 5 minutes on each side, add the Marsala.
Move the scallopine gently around with a fork.
The sauce will become creamy from the amalgam of the flour, butter, and liquid.
Have ready the stock, beef consommé, or water in order to extend the sauce.
(Add more, if necessary, until liquid just covers meat.)
Put lid on pan and let simmer over a low fire for about 10 minutes, which will make the meat more tender.
This dish also seemed to tenderize the hearts of the young ladies who were waiting for me to keep them company.

Veal cutlets sliced thin (¼ pound per person)
Salt
Pepper
2 eggs
Flour
3 tablespoons butter
¼ cup dry Marsala
½ cup stock, beef consommé, or water

## 87  Artichoke omelet

When I came to New York in 1934, I met many Italians. All of them were nostalgic for certain dishes of Italy. We would go to each other's apartments and cook up a taste of home.

Already representing my father in America was Leone Ricci, who had left Florence forty years before. He taught me how to make an artichoke omelet. When we sat down before it, all of us felt as if we were once again in the shadow of Il Duomo.

3 small young artichokes
1 lemon, sliced
4 eggs
Flour
Olive oil
Butter

Slice tops from artichokes and remove hard outside leaves.
Slice artichokes vertically and remove the chokes.
Put artichokes in cold water with 2 slices of lemon, to prevent them from turning black.
Dry slices well and dredge with flour.
Cover bottom of frying pan with olive oil.
When hot, add artichoke slices.
Brown on both sides and then squeeze lemon juice over them.
Using a lid of slightly smaller dimensions than your frying pan, press down on the artichokes.
To increase the pressure, place a weight on top of the lid.
Cook slowly for 2 minutes more.
Butter an ovenproof casserole and line the bottom with artichoke slices.
Warm casserole slightly.
Beat eggs as for an omelet.
Season with salt and pepper.
Pour over artichokes and bake in a moderate oven until eggs are cooked but still soft, approximately 5 to 7 minutes.
Serve at once.
Serves four.

As far as I know, I was the only non-homesick Italian in the whole Italian colony of New York. But I nursed a lot of them who were ill with nostalgia.

Although I was having a marvelous time with Americans, I was delighted to come across an old boyhood chum from Florence, Gianni Puccinelli. Actually, he wasn't so homesick either, since he married an American girl.

Gianni was a wonderful chef and we cooked up some memorable dishes.

## 88  Veal birds

Beat the veal slices with a wooden mallet until paper thin.
Trim away any gristle or fat.
Soak the meat in the beaten eggs for 1 hour.
Sauté the onion in 1 tablespoon of butter until golden.
Set up your pieces of veal in a row on the table.
There should be 12.
On each piece, lay a slice of prosciutto, one leaf of spinach, a pinch of sautéed onion, a slender 3-inch morsel of celery, ½ leaf of sage.
(If fresh sage is available, so much better.)
Roll up tightly your veal birds and secure with string.
If any of the filling exceeds the dimensions of the veal, trim it away so you have a neat package.
Add salt and pepper to flour, dredge the veal rolls well so that during cooking, the flour will not separate from the meat.
Sauté rolls in remainder of ¼ pound butter until well-browned.
Pour on the white wine and let alcohol evaporate.
Stir in the consommé, one cup at a time.

1 pound veal, cut from the
    leg in pieces, 3 by 4 inches
2 eggs
1 onion, chopped
¼ pound butter
½ pound lean prosciutto, cut
    very thin
12 leaves spinach
Celery
6 leaves sage
Salt
Pepper
Flour
½ cup dry white wine
2½ cups beef consommé

*Mashed potatoes*
8 potatoes
Water to cover
4 tablespoons butter
4 tablespoons whole milk
½ cup grated Parmesan cheese
½ cup grated Gruyère cheese

Give the birds an occasional twirl with a fork, so that particles
from the meat will thicken the sauce.
Cover and simmer gently for 30 minutes or until birds are tender.
Meanwhile, boil the potatoes until tender.
Rice them and add butter and hot milk.
Blend in the cheeses.
If dry, add a little hot water.
When the birds are cooked, remove the string and transfer to six
buttered individual ovenproof casseroles, allowing two veal rolls
per person.
Cover the birds in each casserole with a layer of creamy mashed
potatoes.
Set in moderate oven for 10 minutes to brown lightly.
Serve the pan juices in a separate sauce boat.
You can also line up all your veal birds in a single buttered
shallow ovenproof baking dish.
Serves six.

## 89   Fondue Piedmont style

I alway liked the Fontina cheese used for this dish in Torino.
Fortunately the Italian grocers of New York also stocked it.

1 pound Fontina or Gruyère
     cheese
Milk
4 tablespoons butter
4 egg yolks
White pepper
Toast
White truffles

Dice the cheese.
Place in a bowl.
Cover with milk.
Steep for at least 4 hours—longer, if you can.
Melt the butter in a double boiler.
Add the cheese, being careful not to take with it more than ½
teaspoon of milk per person.
Stir well, always in the same direction, until the cheese mixture
spins a thread.

Remove from fire and beat in the egg yolks.
Return to the top of the double boiler and continue stirring until you have achieved a thick cream.
Add a pinch of white pepper.
Serve in pre-heated individual earthenware casseroles (or in one large one) and accompany with a triangle of toast set into the side of each dish.
Cover the surface of the fondue with razor-thin slices of white truffle, one of the great specialties of Piedmont.
Serves six.

———————

Since Amerigo Vespucci and Christopher Columbus went west, there have always been Italians in America. So when I arrived in New York in October, 1934, I already knew so many people up and down the Atlantic seacoast that I might have been born in Philadelphia instead of Florence.

One of my best friends from home was Bill Cini, who had established himself as a silversmith in Boston. Bill was crazy about the lobsters from Maine and didn't see any reason why they couldn't be beautifully combined with spaghetti. He has now transferred his silver workshops to Laguna Beach in California, where, Cini-fashion, he is probably marrying abalone to pasta.

## 90  Lobster Bill

Stun the live lobster by hitting it on the head with a wooden mallet.
Cut it in four sections, taking care to save the liquid.

Sauté until golden the sliced onion and garlic in the olive oil.
Use a deep saucepan.
Remove the garlic clove.
Put the lobster pieces in the pan and add the liquid which you
have put aside plus 2 cups of white wine.
Salt.
Cover and steam for about 10 minutes.
Remove lobster sections and keep warm.
Toss the cooked and drained spaghetti into the pan still
containing the lobster sauce.
Swirl it around, and transfer to a large heated platter.
Pour over any juice that remains in pan.
The lobster pieces you have been keeping warm now go on top
of spaghetti.
Hold back their grabbing hands.
Serves four.

2 small or 1 large lobster
½ onion, sliced
1 clove garlic
2 tablespoons olive oil
2 cups dry white wine
Salt
1 pound spaghetti

---

Another of my Italian friends in those early days in New York
was Mario Gabellini of Rome who worked for Scalamandré Silks.
We used to rush out and go shopping just before the grocers
closed and then prepare a leisurely dinner at home. Gabellini's
onion soup was unlike any I have ever had before. I adopted it
so wholeheartedly, it has now become . . .

## 91  Onion soup, Beppe style

I always start with the principle that I like my onions well
cooked. That's why I don't care for the onion soup in Paris
because the onions are usually underdone.

Brown the onions in the oil and butter over low heat in a large deep-sided sauté pan.
Stir to keep them from sticking.
Count on an hour of stir-frying.
As I said, I like my onions brown.
(Not burned, however.)
Pour on the wine and let evaporate.
Add the consommé and a grind of black pepper.
Cover the pan and simmer for 30 minutes.
Ignite the Cognac and pour into the soup.
Sprinkle the toast thickly with the cheese and dunk briefly each slice into the soup so the cheese will be slightly moist.
Any cheese left over is tossed into the soup.
Ladle the soup into individual earthenware bowls.
Top with a slice of cheese-covered toast.
Set into an oven for 5 minutes, or long enough for the cheese to become golden brown.
Serves eight.

11 cups thickly sliced onions
¼ cup olive oil
2 tablespoons butter
½ cup red wine
8 cups beef consommé
Pepper
Salt to taste
3 tablespoons Cognac
7 or 8 slices of toasted bread
1 cup mixed grated Parmesan
   and Gruyère cheeses

## 92  Peperonata contadina

Another of Gabellini's specialties was a country-style *peperonata*, somewhat similar to the *ratatouille* of the South of France, but with a flavor that suggested Italy rather than Provence. It has a great virtue, because it does not require attention while it is cooking.

Slice unpeeled eggplants vertically ¼ inch thick.
Place on large platter.
Sprinkle with coarse salt.

Cover with a heavy plate and leave for 30 minutes in order to disgorge water and bitterness from the eggplants.

Wash and dry.

Heat olive oil in large pan and add sliced onions and peppers cut in strips.

Sauté slowly.

Drain eggplant slices and dredge with flour which has been seasoned with salt and pepper and put in a paper bag.

Sauté briskly in olive oil in a second pan, turning slices from time to time.

When lightly browned and crisp outside, remove from pan and drain on paper towels.

Continue process until all slices have been fried.

Cut tomatoes in wedges and zucchini in vertical slices.

Now add eggplant, tomatoes and zucchini to the onions and peppers.

Cover and cook slowly for 1 hour or more, stirring occasionally from time to time.

4 eggplants
Coarse salt
½ cup olive oil
2 large onions
3 green, red, and yellow sweet
    peppers
3 large ripe tomatoes
6 small zucchini
Flour
Salt
Pepper

---

Gabellini's *peperonata* has been useful to us in many ways.

Sometimes we make double quantities so we can present it on another day in another fashion.

For instance, a small portion is perfect as an hors d'oeuvre when assembled with cold ham and salami.

A really showy presentation of this essentially country dish is one we saw employed by Maxim's in Paris.

We then adapted it as follows.

Place a generous layer of the *peperonata* in a porcelain serving dish.

Make a series of equidistant depressions in the *peperonata* with the back of spoon.

Carefully slip into each depression a cold poached egg.

Garnish each egg with a piece of red tomato, a leaf of parsley, and coat the entire surface with ⅓ inch of chicken gelatin.

Refrigerate until ready to serve.

Makes as many portions as you have eggs.


This handy friend can also reappear in a wonderful hot dish which I concocted when I returned to Florence to show my friends there that all pasta recipes had not yet been invented.


Place a layer of cooked macaroni in a baking dish.

Cover with a layer of *peperonata*.

Moisten with a little béchamel sauce containing grated Parmesan.

Repeat until you reach the top of the dish.

Heat and serve.

As a variation, you can substitute cubes of mozzarella for the Parmesan.

One of the most important jobs I had in New York in the thirties was to execute some business for my father with an important Swiss banker and industrialist named Werner Abegg. I was young and nervous, because the assignment was a big one. I thought that one of the best ways to establish a rapport with Mr. Abegg was to invite him to the apartment for a lunch. At the time, I knew a beautiful young Canadian girl, Pat Codd, who was working in New York as a photographer's model. She wanted to show me how helpful she could be and insisted on preparing the lunch.

Actually, in those days, Pat was not so experienced in the kitchen, but that did not stop her. That morning she frantically telephoned her mother in Toronto for the family's best recipes.

Pat's first party lunch for me was a tremendous success. Mr. Abegg bought a half interest in a Michelangelo painting.

On that fateful day, lunch was the following:

CONSOMMÉ WITH SHERRY
CHICKEN BAKED IN MILK
SCALLOPED POTATOES
BROCCOLI
PRUNE SOUFFLÉ WITH WHIPPED CREAM

## 93 *Chicken baked in milk*

Shake the chicken (2 pieces at a time) in a paper bag with flour, salt, and pepper, until the chicken is well-floured.
Place chicken in a deep baking dish with a lid.
Quarter the onions and tuck in among the chicken pieces with dabs of butter.
The butter will be the equivalent of a generous tablespoon.
Pour milk to three-quarters of the height of the dish.
Set in hot oven (400° F.).
When milk begins to boil, lower the heat to a minimum and cover the casserole.
Cook slowly for about 1 hour. Remove from oven.
Meanwhile melt 3 tablespoons of butter in a saucepan with 3 tablespoons of flour.
Cook and stir over low heat for 2 minutes.
Strain the liquid from the chicken and add slowly to the flour and butter to form a medium white sauce.
If too thick, dilute with a little warm milk.
Season with salt and pepper.
Pour this sauce over the chicken, separating the pieces delicately with a wooden spoon.
Make sure that each piece is coated with sauce.
Cover the casserole and replace in oven for 10 minutes.
Sauté the sliced mushrooms in 2 tablespoons of butter.
Heat the Cognac in a separate pan, ignite, and pour flaming over the mushrooms while stirring constantly.
At last moment, garnish the chicken with the mushrooms and serve.
A nice accompaniment is scalloped potatoes which bake in the oven at the same time as the chicken.
Serves four.

1 chicken, cut in 8 pieces
Flour
Salt
Pepper
3 medium onions
1½ quarts milk
6 tablespoons butter
3 tablespoons flour
¼ pound mushrooms, sliced
1 tablespoon Cognac

## 94  Scalloped potatoes Myrtle

Peel potatoes and slice thin.
Butter a casserole and arrange a layer of potatoes.
Dot with butter, season with salt and pepper, sprinkle with cornstarch and onions.
Repeat until you have used all the potatoes.
Dot top liberally with butter.
Pour milk until casserole is three-quarters full.
Bake covered 1 hour.
Remove lid and continue baking for 15 to 20 minutes.
Serves four.

6 medium potatoes
3 tablespoons butter
1 teaspoon salt
¼ teaspoon pepper
2 tablespoons cornstarch
2 small white onions
3 cups milk

## 95  Broccoli

Pat learned to cook broccoli from an Italian grocer on Second Avenue. This recipe gives his advice.

Cut off the hard end of the stalks.
Incise bottom of stalks with four gashes.
Tie in small bunches.
Parboil broccoli in large uncovered pot of boiling salted water for 5 minutes.
Drain broccoli in colander.
Cover bottom of same cooking pot with a little olive oil.
Add 1 clove of garlic.
Cook slowly until garlic is golden. Discard garlic.
Put broccoli back into pot.
Cover and cook over very slow heat for about 20 minutes, until stalks are tender when pierced with a fork.

## 96  Prune soufflé

This recipe is so simple sometimes we are ashamed in the face of the effusive compliments.

Pit the prunes and pass through a food mill, but not too fine.
Add sugar and cook together until sugar melts.
Beat egg whites firm.
Add salt and lemon juice and beat again until the egg whites stand in peaks.
Gently fold in the cooled prune mixture and pour into a buttered soufflé dish around which you have set a paper collar.
Bake in preheated moderate oven for 30 minutes.
Remove collar and serve with whipped cream.
Serves four to six.

½ pound prunes, stewed according
    to package directions
½ cup sugar
4 egg whites
¼ teaspoon salt
2 teaspoons lemon juice
1½ cups whipped cream

## 97  Risotto with Shellfish

I married Pat and went to war as a sergeant in the U. S. Army. When I returned to the United States I found many Italian friends who had also been active on the Allied side. Among them was Guido Soro, who has had a brilliant career as Italian Ambassador to Egypt and to Mexico and is now in the Ministry of Foreign Affairs.
In 1947 Soro and I made an informal supper for Ambassador Tarchiani and some of his staff. The shellfish out of Chesapeake Bay were superb. And the recipe the two of us improvised has been a highlight of many of our parties ever since.

Kill the octopus with a blow from a heavy wooden mallet.
Wash it well and cut into strips.
(We know that not everybody likes this kind of work. If you prefer, have the fishmonger kill and cut up the octopus.)

Sauté the strips in a little olive oil, until pale gold.
Cover with dry white wine and bring to a boil.
Put a lid on the pan and simmer for 2 hours.
Wash the clams.
Put in a deep pan, and fill the bottom with ½ inch of liquid made up equally of dry white wine and water.
Cover and steam until clams open.
Remove from fire and separate meat from shells.
Drain off juice and save.
Peel shrimps and sauté in a little butter.
Sauté onions in butter until golden in deep pot.
Add rice.
Stir.
Little by little add the strained liquid from the octopus and the clams.
After 15 minutes, add the octopus and the shrimps and continue until rice is cooked.
If you are short of liquid, add hot water.
At the last minute, toss in the shelled clams.
Remove pot from the stove and blend with the whipped cream.
Pour Cognac in small pan, ignite, and mix with this ambrosial *risotto*.
Serves six to eight.

1 1½-pound octopus
3 tablespoons olive oil
4 tablespoons dry white wine
2 dozen small clams
½ pound scampi or shrimps
1 onion, chopped fine
Butter
1 pound rice
3 tablespoons whipped cream
Cognac

Pasta Festival

For the 1969 Fair, my friend, Pietro Barilla, was one of the chief advisers for the gastronomic side. Barilla is one of the foremost manufacturers of pasta in Italy. So we presented some of the most popular and interesting pasta dishes in our national repertory.

PENNE ALLA CARBONARA

MACARONI WITH EGGPLANT

BEAN SOUP

THIN NOODLES WITH PESTO

SPAGHETTI ALL'AMATRICIANA

SPAGHETTI ALLE VONGOLE BEPPE STYLE

BAKED TAGLIATELLE WITH VEGETABLES

GRANNY CONCETTA'S TORTELLINI

GRANNY CONCETTA'S MEAT SAUCE

MACARONI WITH OLD ARMAGNAC

DELIZIE VERDI

LA CARMAGNOLA

SPAGHETTI SHOESTRING POTATOES

PASTA ALL'ANTIQUARIA

SPAGHETTI PIZZA

FUSILLI IN WALNUT SAUCE

PASTA SHELLS WITH PEPPERS

## 98  *Penne alla carbonara*

Since Italy is not a coal-producing country, charcoal was always important. The person who fabricates charcoal is called a *carbonaro*. The famous method of preparing any kind of pasta *alla carbonara* was developed by the charcoal makers.

Place the bacon and peeled clove of garlic in a heavy skillet.
Cover with first quality olive oil.
(This may seem like a lot of olive oil, but have confidence.)
Cook over low flame.
Remove garlic as soon as browned.
When bacon is done, but not crisp, take pan from fire and allow to cool.
In a large bowl, big enough to later contain the pasta, put the 7 egg yolks.
(Always calculate 1 egg yolk per person and an additional yolk for the pot.)
Stir the yolks with a fork.
Do not beat.
Add the grated pecorino and Parmesan and blend well together.
Pour in the cream.
When oil and bacon are sufficiently cooled, add to the egg and cheese mixture.
Stir well.
The process to this point can be done hours before using.
When ready, cook your *penne* in boiling salted water.
Drain and toss into the bowl of *carbonara* sauce which will be

¼ pound lean bacon, diced
1 clove garlic
7 egg yolks
⅔ cup grated Parmesan
⅓ cup grated pecorino, Romano, or
    any sharp cheese
2 tablespoons cream
2 tablespoons olive oil
1 pound *penne* (small *rigatoni*)
Salt
Pepper
Paprika

warmed up by the heat of the pasta.
Season with salt, pepper, and paprika.
However, if your bacon is salty, add no more salt.
The paprika provides a brave dash of color.
Serves six.

## 99   Macaroni with eggplant

Cut the eggplant in ¼ inch slices and sprinkle with salt.
Let them drain for about 30 minutes. Wash well and dry.
Then flour with seasoned flour the slices and deep fry in oil and
put aside on paper towels.
Make a béchamel sauce.
Melt 2 tablespoons butter and add 2 tablespoons flour.
Cook 2 minutes.
Add milk, salt, pepper and Parmesan.
Cook the macaroni in a lot of boiling salted water until they are
*al dente.*
Drain, and in a buttered deep ovenware dish, place layers of
macaroni, eggplant, mozzarella, and béchamel until all is used up.
Bake in moderate oven for about 45 minutes or until well
browned on top.
Serves six.

3 eggplants
Salt
3 tablespoons flour
2 cups oil
2 tablespoons butter
2 tablespoons flour
4 cups milk
1 tablespoon salt
1 teaspoon pepper
1 cup grated Parmesan cheese
1 pound macaroni
½ pound mozzarella cheese, cut
    in small pieces

## 100 Bean soup

Soak the beans and cook slowly in very little water.
In a deep casserole, prepare the *soffritto* as follows.
Pour in the olive oil and add the onion, garlic, and the rosemary (stripped from the stalk).
When the onion is golden brown, add the tomatoes, salt, and pepper and cook for about 20 minutes.
Into this purée go the beans and the water in which they were cooked plus 9 additional cups of water.
Simmer, partially covered, for 2 hours or more.
Add the pasta, which has been cooked apart.
Serve with a side dish of grated Parmesan.
Some people top their soup with a spoonful or two of fresh olive oil.
Serves six.

½ pound dried white beans
⅔ cup olive oil
1 medium onion, chopped
2 cloves garlic, chopped
1 sprig rosemary
½ cup peeled tomatoes
9 cups water
1½ cups cooked pasta (shells, elbow, *rigatoni*, or any short pasta)
1 tablespoon salt
½ teaspoon pepper
Parmesan cheese

## 101 Thin noodles with pesto

*Trenette* is a dish you will always find in the charming resort of Portofino on the Ligurian coast. *Trenette* is a Genoese version of long thin flat noodle, about the thickness of a matchstick.
*Pesto* is their marvelous sauce of fresh basil. Together they make the most sublime pasta combination in all Italy. We are far from alone in this opinion.

Peel the potatoes and cut in small pieces.
Cook in boiling salted water to cover for 10 to 15 minutes.
Do not overcook.
Drain well and dry them out in heated saucepan.

1 pound *trenette* (thin noodles)
¼ pound fresh green string beans
2 medium potatoes

String the beans and slice on the diagonal in thirds.
Plunge into boiling salted water just to cover and cook 10 to 12 minutes.
They should still have some crispness left. Drain.
Cook the *trenette* in an enormous quantity of boiling salted water for 10 minutes.
They will still be chewy or *al dente*. Drain well.
Toss together the potatoes, beans, pasta and the *pesto* so that the noodles, potatoes, and beans are all well coated.
Sprinkle abundantly with grated Parmesan.

Fresh basil leaves, 1 large bouquet or more
1 handful pine nuts, roasted in oven
2 cloves garlic
2 tablespoons grated Sardinian pecorino cheese
4 tablespoons grated Parmesan
1 cup olive oil
Coarse salt

*Pesto*

Pound in a marble mortar with a wooden pestle the basil leaves, pine nuts, cloves of garlic, and a pinch of coarse cooking salt.
The coarse salt keeps the basil green.
Add the cheese and stir until all is well mixed into a thick purée.
Transfer to a bowl and pour the oil drop by drop in a gentle stream mixing steadily until you have obtained a creamy mixture.
When it is the consistency of soft butter, toss it on the steaming mound of *trenette*.
Should the paste be too thick, you can thin it with a little more olive oil.
If you have any *pesto* left over, you can always keep it in the refrigerator, covering the top with a thin film of olive oil.
Serves six.

Because this sauce is pretty close to heaven, we never have enough, much less any left over. In Liguria, *pesto* is often added to a minestrone, which improves it immeasurably. Elisabeth David, the English gastronome, suggests *pesto* instead of butter on baked potatoes.

## 102 *Spaghetti all'Amatriciana*

Originally this simple appetizing dish came from the mountainous region of the Abruzzo. Some years ago it was adopted by the Romans and you will find it in every *trattoria*. In fact it was brought by Abruzzi boys who came to Rome to work as waiters. These days since everybody goes to *trattorie*, Spaghetti all'Amatriciana is becoming increasingly popular.

Cover the bottom of a cast iron frying pan with olive oil.
Sauté garlic until golden.
Discard.
In the same pan try out the salt pork and fry the onion until pale gold.
Pour in the wine.
Cook until evaporated.
Add the tomatoes, salt, and pepper.
Cook over fast flame for only 5 minutes, so that the tomatoes retain their fresh taste.
Add a handful chopped parsley at last minute.
This is optional but the green enhances the red color of the tomatoes.

Meanwhile, cook the spaghetti in plenty of boiling, well-salted water.
Strain and as soon as it is in a hot dish, pour the sauce over it.
Sprinkle with Parmesan and the pecorino.
Serves four.

Olive oil
2 cloves garlic
¼ pound salt pork or bacon, diced
3 tablespoons chopped onion
¼ cup dry white wine
1 pound ripe tomatoes, peeled
    and cut into pieces
3 or 4 sprigs parsley, chopped
    (optional)
1 pound spaghetti
¼ cup grated Parmesan cheese
¼ cup grated pecorino or any
    other sharp cheese
Salt
Pepper

## 103   Spaghetti with clams, Beppe style

Scrub clams under running water to clean.
Sauté onion and garlic in olive oil until pale gold using deep saucepan.
Put in clams and the dry white wine.
When the wine starts to boil, lower heat, and cover pan.
Steam until clams open, discarding any which have remained shut.
Take out clams and shell.
Toss drained and cooked spaghetti into the liquid in the saucepan.
Stir well.
Add shelled clams and parsley.
Add salt and pepper to taste.
Mix.
Serve on heated platter.
Serves six.

2 pounds small hard-shelled clams
1 onion, chopped
1 clove garlic, minced
4 tablespoons olive oil
2 cups dry white wine
1 pound spaghetti, cooked and
   drained
2 tablespoons minced parsley
Salt
Pepper

## 104   Baked tagliatelle with vegetables

Cook green peas, spinach, and snap beans.
(Keep the water in which the vegetables are cooked.)
Chop roughly the spinach and the beans.
Prepare a béchamel sauce with ½ cup flour, 2 tablespoons butter, 2 cups milk and 2 cups cream.
Add ½ cup grated Parmesan cheese, ½ cup grated Gruyère cheese, and nutmeg.
Sauté the vegetables in 2 tablespoons butter and add them to the béchamel sauce together with the vegetable water.
Mix well and bring to the boil.

1 pound fresh green peas in pods,
   shelled
1 pound fresh spinach, washed and
   drained
1 pound fresh snap beans, washed
   and drained
½ cup flour
4 tablespoons butter
2 cups milk
2 cups cream
½ cup grated Parmesan cheese
½ cup grated Gruyère cheese
¼ teaspoon nutmeg

When it boils, add the pasta and cook it together.
Put the mixture in a buttered fireproof dish, sprinkle with bread crumbs, and brown in the oven.
Serves eight.

4 cups water in which vegetables
    were cooked
¾ pound *tagliatelle* made with eggs
    and cut in 1½-inch-wide strips
Bread crumbs

## 105   Granny Concetta's tortellini

*Method* (or as Granny would say, what you should do to make them):
Put the flour on the pastry board and work the eggs into the flour.
Work the pastry until it is soft and smooth and then begin to knead it.
(It takes Granny's hands to get the dough thin.
However, do your best!)
Roll out dough until it is very thin.
Remember to keep it in a cool damp place so that it does not harden and become dry.
Next cut the dough into 3-inch squares and put just enough filling in the center of each square so that when second square is put on top, the *tortellino* can be sealed around the edges.
It is difficult to explain just how to get the exact form of the Bolognese *tortellino* unless you have a Granny Concetta at hand to give you a practical demonstration.
However, even if the shape is not perfect, if you follow the instructions for the filling (for which you should use plenty of the best ingredients), the end result will be good anyway.

*Ingredients for the pasta:*
1½ pounds flour
6 eggs

*The filling:*

In a mortar grind with pestle the sirloin, the ham, the mortadella, and the turkey very fine (Granny will not hear of using a grinder even though, in our opinion, this would simplify matters considerably).
Put the ground meat into a bowl; add the eggs, grated cheese, marrow, nutmeg and work together until the texture is even and the color is golden.

Points to remember for a perfect success:
The filling should be made the day before the *tortellini*, and the *tortellini* should be made the day before they are to be eaten. The various ingredients have thus the opportunity to amalgamate.
The filling—so Granny says—should be kept for a day outside the window in the cold (Granny only makes *tortellini* for Christmas and for the New Year—probably because she has never been able to afford them more often and, besides, she has a marked aversion for refrigerators, which, she says, make the sort of cold she does not like).

*Ingredients for the filling:*
½ pound sirloin of pork
¼ pound Parma ham
¼ pound mortadella sausage
¼ pound breast of turkey
2 eggs
2 ounces beef marrow
Nutmeg
Salt
½ pound extra-old Parmesan cheese (*stravecchio*), grated

## Granny Concetta's meat sauce

Chop the carrot, celery, onion, and bacon finely and fry until lightly colored.
When the bacon is a golden brown, add the pork finely chopped—and the giblets (add the liver last as it is the tenderest).
When everything is nicely colored add about ½ cup of milk and

1 carrot
1 stalk celery
1 onion
⅓ pound salted bacon
½ pound sirloin of pork
Giblets of old hen
½ cup milk
Tomato paste or canned tomatoes
1 cup consommé

144

when this is completely absorbed add the tomatoes or the tomato paste together with a cup of consommé.

Simmer for about 3 hours, adding hot consommé if it becomes too dry.

If possible use a terracotta cooking pot.

Serves eight.

———————————

One day Beppe was wondering whether most Americans really liked pasta. I told him that the American taste for spaghetti and macaroni goes back a long time. When Thomas Jefferson became President of the United States, he requested his chargé d'affaires to drop down to Naples some time and send him a macaroni-making machine for use in the White House.

This conversation led us to Beppe's friend, Siso Pizzetti, head of the Braibanti factory for pasta, who has made a hobby of collecting sumptuous recipes using all forms of noodles. Mr. Pizzetti generously turned over a few of his favorite recipes.

## 106  Macaroni with old Armagnac

Chop the onion, celery, carrot, and parsley.

Sauté gently in a pan with the olive oil.

In another frying pan, melt the butter and add the tomatoes.

Add salt and sugar.

When the tomatoes have begun to disintegrate, pour on the old Armagnac.

Cook for several minutes.

1 medium onion
½ stalk celery
½ carrot
3 sprigs parsley
¾ cup olive oil
2 tablespoons butter
6 tomatoes, peeled
Salt
1 teaspoon sugar
¼ cup old Armagnac
1¼ pounds *labirinti* (short macaroni)
Freshly ground black pepper

Transfer the onion, celery, carrot, and parsley to the tomatoes.
Simmer together for 10 minutes.
Pour the sauce over cooked, drained macaroni.
Toss well together.
Serve in a mound on a silver platter.
Grind fresh black pepper over the macaroni at the table.
Serves six.


## 107   Green delights

Partially cook the *lasagnoni* (large sheets of green *lasagne*) in boiling salted water for about 6 minutes.
Drain on a clean kitchen towel.
Prepare the filling as follows: mix in a bowl the mozzarella cut into small cubes, the prosciutto cut in pieces (do not remove the fat), the egg yolks, and the béchamel.
Spread the filling over the drained sheets of *lasagnoni*.
Roll up and lay side by side in a buttered rectangular ovenproof dish.
Cover with the meat sauce and the dried mushrooms which have been plumped in water and then dried and sautéed in butter.
Season with salt and pepper.
Moisten with 2 tablespoons of Marsala.
Dab with butter.
Set in a moderate oven for 10 minutes or until well gratinéed.
Garnish with small whole mushrooms and bits of cooked ham sautéed together in butter.
At moment of serving, sprinkle liberally with grated Parmesan.
Serves six.
*Note:* If *lasagnoni* are not available, you can make this dish with ordinary *lasagne*.

½ pound green *lasagnoni* (made with egg and spinach)
1 pound mozzarella
¼ pound prosciutto
5 egg yolks
2 cups thick béchamel
2 cups meat sauce (alla Bolognese)
¼ pound dried mushrooms
¼ pound butter
Salt
Pepper
2 tablespoons Marsala
12 small whole mushrooms
2 slices cooked ham, diced
⅓ pound grated Parmesan cheese

## 108  La carmagnola

Cook the pasta in boiling salted water until *al dente*, 6 to 7 minutes.
Drain well and return to the cooking pot.
Add milk, 1 tablespoon of cream and the butter.
Cook for 2 minutes over very low flame, turning with a wooden spoon.
Add the grated Parmesan, salt, a few grinds of black pepper, and a pinch of nutmeg.
Turn for another minute or two until the pasta is well coated with the cheese.
Have the meat balls ready, prepared as follows.
Mix the ground veal with egg and Parmesan and moisten with the Cognac.
Sauté in butter until browned on all sides.
Arrange a heap of cooked pasta and the miniature meat balls.
Sprinkle with white truffle.
Serves six.

1¼ pounds of *messicani* or *rigatoni*
2 tablespoons milk
4 tablespoons cream
¼ pound butter
½ pound grated Parmesan cheese
Salt
Pepper
Nutmeg
2 dozen miniature meat balls
   prepared with:
½ pound ground veal
1 egg
4 tablespoons grated Parmesan
   cheese
Salt
Pepper
¼ cup Cognac
White truffle, sliced razor thin

## 109  Spaghetti with matchstick potatoes

The idea of combining spaghetti with shoestring potatoes is so audacious that most people might hold back. However, if you are willing to dare such a binge, you will find the combination delicious.

Pare the potatoes and cut in matchsticks.
Soak in ice cold water.
Drain.
Dry well.

4 potatoes
1 pound thin spaghetti
¼ pound butter
1 cup grated Parmesan cheese
Peanut oil

Cook the spaghetti in a large quantity of boiling, salted water.
Drain and return to cooking pot with the butter and the grated Parmesan.
Meanwhile deep fry the matchstick potatoes in the peanut oil.
Drain on paper towels.
Toss quickly into the spaghetti.
The potatoes should offer the contrast of crispness.
Forget to count the calories.
Serves six.

## 110  Pasta all'antiquaria

Beppe improvised this recipe for the popular Italian gastronomic magazine, *La Cucina Italiana*. The magazine baptized it: "Pasta all'Antiquaria."

Brown the onions in the butter and oil over very low heat.
Stir from time to time to prevent them from sticking.
Simmer for 1 hour.
Pour on the wine.
Let evaporate.
Add the Cognac and ignite.
Boil the *penne* in a large quantity of salted water for 6 minutes.
Drain and return to cooking pot with 1 cup of béchamel and ½ cup grated Parmesan.
Toss well together for a minute over low heat.
Butter a large ovenproof casserole or baking dish.
Spread a layer of *penne*.
Sprinkle with grated Parmesan and dot with butter.
Add a layer of onions.

10 onions, thickly sliced
1 pound *penne* (small *rigatoni*)
2 tablespoons olive oil
1 tablespoon butter
½ cup white wine
2 tablespoons Cognac
2 cups thin béchamel
3 tablespoons butter
1 cup grated Parmesan cheese

Continue alternating layers of *penne*, cheese, and onions ending with a layer of *penne*.
Pour on the remaining cup of béchamel.
Sprinkle with a little paprika.
Heat in moderate oven for 12 to 15 minutes.
At moment of serving, top with a sprinkling of grated Parmesan.
Serves six.

## 113   Pasta shells with peppers

Remove the seeds and filaments from the peppers and cut in strips.
If you can find red, yellow, and green peppers, the effect is quite colorful.
Otherwise, use all green peppers.
Peel, seed, and dice the tomatoes.
Slice thinly the onion.
Cover the bottom of a frying pan with oil and a little butter.
Sauté the onion slices until pale gold.
Add the peppers and cook over a fairly high flame, stirring frequently.
When the peppers begin to become tender, add the tomatoes, a generous bunch of basil, salt, and pepper. Lower the flame.
Cover the pan and cook for about 15 minutes.
Remove the lid and allow water from the tomatoes to evaporate.
While the pepper and tomatoes are simmering, cook the pasta shells *al dente* and drain well.
Combine with the pepper and tomato mixture.
Sprinkle generously with grated Parmesan.
Serves four to five.

1 pound pasta shells
1 pound sweet peppers
1 pound tomatoes
1 onion
Basil
Salt
Pepper
Oil
Butter
Grated Parmesan cheese

# Beppe's Favorite Recipes

# Menu XIX

AVOCADO SOUP

AVOCADO SOUP COLD

SCALLOPINE WITH LEMON

QUENELLES DE DORE

LOBSTER SAUCE

SNAILS ALLA CORTONA

FRESH TUNA WITH PEAS

GUIDO'S HALF MOONS

BISCOTTI DI PRATO (TATINI)

COCKTAIL CHEESE BISCUITS

FLORENTINE SPONGECAKE

## 114  Avocado soup

Peel and slice the avocados.
Pour over lemon juice to keep them from discoloring. Put aside.
Sauté the sliced onions in butter until pale gold.
Add the broth.
Season with pepper, cayenne, paprika, and salt.
When the soup comes to the boil, add the avocados sliced.
Simmer for 2 or 3 minutes.
Serves six.

2 avocados
2 tablespoons lemon juice
½ cup sliced onion
2 tablespoons butter
6 cups chicken broth
¼ tablespoon pepper
¼ teaspoon cayenne pepper
¼ teaspoon paprika
½ teaspoon salt

## 115  Avocado soup cold

Cool the hot avocado soup.
Place, one cup at a time, in the blender.
Whir for 30 seconds.
Serve well chilled in bouillon cups, garnished with sliced black olives.
Serves six.

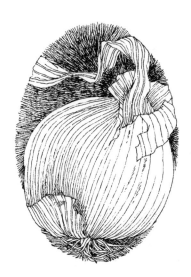

## 116 Scallopine with lemon

Soak scallops in beaten egg for 1 hour.
Pat well with flour.
Season with salt and pepper.
Brown slowly on both sides in butter.
Add wine.
Let evaporate.
Pour on broth and lemon juice.
Cover.
Simmer for 20 minutes.
During last 5 minutes add chopped parsley.
Swirl the sauce and serve.
Serves eight.

2 pounds veal scallops, pounded
    very thin
1 egg, beaten
Flour
6 tablespoons butter
Salt
Pepper
¼ cup dry white wine
½ cup chicken broth
Juice of 1 lemon
½ cup chopped parsley

## 117 Quenelles of sea bream

When I went to the Expo '67 in Montreal, Gerald Bronfman, the Canadian financier, served us these exquisite quenelles in his beautiful office overlooking the old city.

Put fish and fat through meat grinder.
Beat in white of egg with a wooden spoon.
Add cream slowly.
Mix well and form into 8 balls the size of an egg.
Place in a greased pan.
Add white wine.
Cover and cook slowly for 10 minutes.

1 pound sea bream fillets
    (remove any bones)
¼ pound beef kidney fat
1 egg white
¼ cup heavy cream
¼ cup dry white wine

## 118   Lobster sauce

Fry carrot, onion, celery, and garlic in the oil until golden brown.
Add lobster pieces.
Cook until lobster turns red.
Pour on Cognac and flame.
Stir in tomatoes, white wine, flour, and let cook slowly for about
20 minutes.
Remove lobster.
Put sauce through a fine strainer.
Simmer for 5 minutes.
Add lobster meat from the shell and the cream.
Cook slowly for 15 minutes.
Season with salt and pepper.
Serve over quenelles.
Serves four.

1 carrot, finely chopped
1 medium onion, chopped
2 branches celery, chopped
1 small clove garlic
¼ cup vegetable oil
1 live lobster cut in pieces
1 ounce Cognac
1 cup stewed tomatoes
1 cup white wine
1 tablespoon flour
1 cup light cream

## 119   Snails alla Cortona

First a little bit of history about snails, as it pertains to our part
of the world.
A certain Fulvius Harpinius was supposed to have had a large
farm for fattening snails on the outskirts of Pompeii. Thousands
of them were found in the area after the famous eruption. Latin
had a word for the snail, the *scarabaeus*. From it was derived the
French word, *escargot*.
Pliny describes them as being a delicacy at Roman feasts,
informing us that the best came from Sicily, Capri, and the
Balearics. The largest came from Illyria. Numbers existed on the

Ligurian coast. The ships brought them down to satisfy the large demand among Roman gourmets.

Today, they are a specialty of the little medieval town of Cortona, near Arezzo.

Only a purist would clean the snails himself. The lazy, like most of us, would buy the snails in cans. However, this is the way they must be prepared by purists.

Place the snails in a cloth-covered basket with 2 tablespoons of bran.
Leave them for 4 days to purge themselves.
Wash several times in cold running water.
Cover with plenty of water, the vinegar, and the salt.
Disturb them every now and then.
Change the salted vinegar water several times, until the last traces of scum disappear.
Place the cleaned snails in a large saucepan with 1 garlic clove, 1 peeled whole onion, 1 stalk celery.
Cover with water.
Cook slowly for 4 hours.
Put ½ cup olive oil in a saucepan.
Add 3 chopped cloves of garlic, 1 chopped onion, 1 chopped stalk of celery, 4 tablespoons chopped parsley.
Brown lightly.
Add the tomatoes, the tomato paste, 3 cups of water.
Cook for 10 minutes.
Add the pepper and the chopped fillets of anchovy.
Add the snails to this sauce.
Cook covered over low heat for 2 hours.
Stir from time to time.
Serve hot in the shells.
Serves four to six.

3 pounds snails
2 cups vinegar
½ pound coarse salt
4 cloves garlic
2 onions
2 stalks celery
4 tablespoons chopped parsley
2 tomatoes, peeled and chopped
2 tablespoons tomato paste
4 anchovy fillets
½ cup olive oil
Pepper

## 120  Fresh tuna with peas

Cut tuna into 1-inch-thick slices.
Brown clove of garlic in olive oil and discard; sauté the slices of tuna in the oil, add parsley, salt, and pepper.
Turn over the slices and add the diluted tomato paste and bay leaves.
When the slices are cooked, take them out, add fresh peas, and cook them in the sauce.
Add more water if the sauce becomes too thick.
When the peas are cooked, put tuna slices back in the pan. As soon as they are heated through, serve immediately.
Serves eight.

2 pounds fresh tuna (or any firm-fleshed fish)
2 cloves garlic
½ cup olive oil
1 bunch parsley
1 teaspoon salt
½ teaspoon pepper
2 tablespoons tomato paste diluted in 1 cup water
2 bay leaves
2 cups shelled peas

## 121  Guido's half moons

Dissolve the yeast in the warm water.
Add the flour and knead well.
Form into a ball.
Set in bowl.
Cover with towel.
Let rise in warm place for 45 minutes.
Roll until thin on floured pastry board.
Cut into 2-inch circles.
Top ⅓ of the rounds with mozzarella, ⅓ with prosciutto, ⅓ with boiled ham.
Fold over to form miniature half moons.
Prick a few holes with the tines of a fork.
Deep fry in very hot oil or fat.
Serve immediately.

2 teaspoons yeast
Warm water to mix
1 pound flour
½ cup chopped mozzarella
⅔ cup raw chopped prosciutto
⅔ cup chopped cooked ham
Salt

You can vary the fillings with anchovies, chopped spinach mixed with ricotta, chopped mushrooms, etc., ad infinitum.

These half moons are a delight at a cocktail party.

## 122   Cocktail cheese biscuits

Cut butter into flour.
Add Parmesan, salt, and pepper and if needed, a little water.
Knead on floured board just enough so dough holds together.
Roll out to about ½ inch thickness.
Cut in shapes with pastry cutter.
Put in moderate oven (350° F.) for 15 to 20 minutes or until they are golden brown.
They can be kept for several weeks in an airtight tin box.
Reheat when ready to serve.
Serves twelve.

1 pound butter
1½ pounds flour
½ pound Parmesan cheese, grated
Salt
Pepper

## 123   Biscotti di Prato (Tatini)

Beppe obtained the recipe for these typical Florentine cookies from Tatini, a confectioner who has a small bakeshop near his house.

Sift together flour and baking powder.
Add the sugar, 2 eggs, salt, and the almonds broken into small bits.
Mix well together and form into two long skinny loaves.
Brush surface with 1 beaten egg.
Bake in slow oven for 20 minutes.

3 cups flour
1 teaspoon baking powder
1½ cups sugar
3 eggs
Pinch of salt
½ pound shelled almonds

Cut on the diagonal in ½ inch slices.
These biscotti become very hard and keep for weeks.
They are meant to be eaten dipped in sweet red wine.
By eating too many cookies, we have become quite tipsy.

## 124   Florentine spongecake

Tatini also divulged his recipe for this local spongecake.

Dissolve yeast in warm water.
Add to flour.
Mix well.
Let rise for 20 minutes.
Combine the ingredients of the second mixture and knead with the first until you achieve an elastic dough.
Place in a baking tin.
When it has risen a little, set in a moderate oven (350° F.) for 15 to 20 minutes.
Sprinkle with confectioners' sugar and serve.

*First mixture:*
2 tablespoons yeast
¼ cup water
1 cup flour

*Second mixture:*
1 cup flour
⅓ cup sugar
½ cup vegetable shortening
1 egg
Pinch of salt
1 teaspoon grated orange rind
Confectioners' sugar

Naomi on Her Own

Most of my Italian cooking has been done in Porto Ercole, a sardine fishing port on the southern tip of Tuscany, which has become a favorite summer resort with Florentines. The terrace of my apartment overlooking the port has become a gathering place at cocktail hour because it is the best place in town to watch the colorful *passeggiata*. From 6 P.M. until 8 P.M. everybody walks up and down. The clothes are glorious and so are the people. The view from the terrace is like a loge at the theater.

As an accompaniment to drinks, I decided to experiment with stuffed flowers of zucchini. I remembered them with delight, having tasted them at the restaurant Augusteo in Rome. My version took four days of trial and error. They were such a success that three bunches of flowers were gone before I had time to get out of the kitchen.

The following recipe is in the old-fashioned manner, meaning without exact quantities, because the size of the flowers determines the amount of filling. I can assure you, however, that you will never have any left over, no matter how many you make. The stuffing may be prepared ahead of time, so that only the deep frying need to be done at the last minute.

STUFFED FLOWERS OF ZUCCHINI

EGGPLANT CAVIAR

IMAM BAYILDI

EGGPLANT CALABRESE

MOUSSAKAS HORIS KREAS OR
    MEATLESS MOUSSAKA

BAKED SEA BASS

STUFFED PEPPERS PASSETTO

MINIATURE PIZZA

## 125 Stuffed flowers of zucchini

Make a paste of ½ mozzarella, ¼ gorgonzola, and ¼ grated
Parmesan.
Season with a few grinds of the pepper mill.
Thin with a little milk.
Pack this mixture into a pastry tube.
Fill the zucchini flowers.
The petals of the flowers should be well-closed over the filling.
If you are nimble-fingered, you can tie them together like the
ends of a bandanna.
To make the batter, whip the egg whites until foamy and fold
them into a well-beaten egg yolk.
Lighten with a little beer.
Dip the stuffed flowers into this mixture, and then coat them with
flour.
Deep fry in very hot peanut oil, turning them over so that they
are nicely browned and crisped on all sides.
This should not take more than a minute or a minute and a half.
Remove with a slotted spoon.
Drain on paper toweling.
Serve at once.

Mozzarella
Gorgonzola
Grated Parmesan cheese
Pepper
Milk
30 fresh flowers of zucchini

*Batter:*
1 egg yolk
2 egg whites
Beer
Flour
Peanut oil

The above filling produces a particularly felicitous texture when
deep-fried. However, the procedure couldn't be more onerous, even
if you pack the stuffing into the flower shells with your pinkie
finger.

However, a happy simplification can be obtained by inserting small cubes of mozzarella dusted with black pepper, a snippet of well-washed anchovy fillet, and a sprinkle of grated Parmesan.

The eggplants in the vegetable stalls of Porto Ercole are a feast for the eye. There are the long variety, opulently curved at the base with seductive shining deep purple skins. The round ones are a combination of pageant colors—purple striated with white at the neck.
People buy them for the sheer joy of piling them in a bowl. The more talented paint or photograph them. Since you can't resist buying them every morning that you pass the market, eventually you decide it might be a good idea to cook them as well. Every time I made cold eggplant salad, or eggplant caviar, as it is sometimes called for a first course, I found that eager guests had already consumed most of it as a dip with small crackers. It is delicious, no matter when you eat it.

## 126   *Eggplant caviar*

Bake the eggplants in a moderate oven until the skins shrivel and the flesh is soft inside.
This takes about an hour.
When cooled, scoop out the flesh and mash well in a bowl.
Quickly work in the lemon juice, which keeps the eggplant from discoloring.
Add the well-grated onion and the tomato which has been skinned by plunging into hot water and then chopped finely.
Carefully pour on the best quality of olive oil, but only to the

3 pounds eggplant, long or round
2 tablespoons lemon juice
2 tablespoons grated onion
1 large ripe tomato
Olive oil
Salt
Pepper
½ teaspoon oregano
¼ teaspoon wine vinegar

point that it can be absorbed by the mashed eggplants.
One cup is usually the right amount but more can be added if
the eggplant can take it.
Season with salt, pepper, and oregano.
Stir in ¼ teaspoon of wine vinegar.
Mix and chill.
Arrange in a wide shallow bowl and decorate with a ring of
alternating tomato wedges and strips of green pepper.
Serves six to eight.


## 127   Imam Bayildi

One of the most glorious uses of eggplant as an hors d'oeuvre is
Imam Bayildi. This dish is of Turkish origin. The legend has it
that the Imam had important guests for dinner one day. The cook
wanted to do his boss proud so he invented a new preparation.
When the Imam tasted it, he fainted with delight.
I have come across a number of recipes for the swooning Imam.
The following method for 6 persons had my guests in transports.
Imam Bayildi should be prepared several hours before you plan to
serve it.

Cook the eggplants in a large uncovered pot of rapidly boiling
water for 5 minutes.
Turn them over from time to time with a wooden spoon so you
don't pierce the skin.
If necessary, use two pots.
If the eggplants are too crowded they might become bruised when
turned.
Plunge into cold water to cool quickly.

3 medium large eggplants
2 onions
1 green pepper
4 ripe medium tomatoes
6 tablespoons olive oil
1 clove garlic, minced
1½ teaspoons salt
½ teaspoon sugar
¼ teaspoon oregano
⅛ teaspoon freshly ground
    black pepper
2 tablespoons lemon juice
2 tablespoons chopped parsley
¼ cup pine nuts

Split the eggplants in half lengthwise.

Cut around the inside of each half, leaving ½-inch shell of flesh around the bottoms and edges.

Cut the pulp into small dice and carefully remove, trying not to pierce the skin.

Place the eggplant shells, skin side up, on a dish covered with paper towels.

Chill.

They will look like a disaster at this point. However, later when filled, the shape will be restored.

Peel the onions and slice thinly.

Cut the green pepper in half, remove seeds, and cut into thin julienne strips.

Put 3 tablespoons olive oil in a large skillet.

Sauté the sliced onions and the pepper strips until just wilted, about 5 minutes.

Add the garlic and the diced eggplant.

Cover and cook over low heat for an additional 7 minutes, giving an occasional stir.

Add the salt, sugar, oregano, and pepper.

Stir and cook for about 2 minutes more.

Remove from stove.

Plunge the tomatoes into boiling water for about 30 seconds.

Remove cores, slip off skins, cut into halves, and scrape out the seeds.

Drain on paper towels.

Cut into small chunks.

Gently stir the uncooked tomato chunks into the eggplant, onion, and green pepper mixture which has been transferred to a large bowl.

Mix in the remaining 3 tablespoons of olive oil and the 2 tablespoons of lemon juice.

Chill well for 3 to 4 hours.

Just before serving, pat the inside of the eggplant shells dry with a paper towel.

Using a slotted spoon, divide the vegetable mixture among the shells, heaping as high as necessary.

Sprinkle each eggplant half with the parsley and the pine nuts.

Serves six.


## 128   *Eggplant Calabrese*

A maid who was born in Calabria enlarged our Porto Ercole repertory by preparing for lunch one day a Calabrese casserole of eggplant and tomatoes.

3 pounds round eggplants
Salt
Flour
Oil
1 large onion, peeled
3 pounds egg tomatoes
1 tablespoon fresh basil
1 tablespoon fresh parsley
1 mozzarella cheese
Grated Parmesan cheese
4 hard-boiled eggs

Slice the eggplants.

Cover with salt to drain off any bitterness.

Leave for 30 minutes.

Wash and dry well.

Flour the eggplant slices.

Deep fry lightly in very hot oil.

Drain on paper towels.

Cut the onion and tomatoes into chunks.

Toss into a deep casserole with the basil and parsley and a little salt.

Cover with 2 tablespoons olive oil.

Simmer for 30 minutes.

Pass the sauce through a sieve.

In a large flat baking dish, spread a layer of fried eggplant slices, thin slices of mozzarella, a generous grating of Parmesan, and tomato sauce.

Repeat.

On the top layer, arrange slices of hard-boiled egg.

Dot with cheese and moisten liberally with sauce.

Bake in a moderate oven for 15 minutes.

Serves six to eight.

For a more refined version, substitute ricotta cheese for mozzarella.

## 129   Moussakas horis kreas or Meatless moussaka

One of my Porto Ercole guests went off to Greece for a few days' vacation and returned with this excellent recipe.

Slice 2 pounds of eggplant.

Salt and allow to rest for 30 minutes.

Rinse and dry.

Fry lightly and quickly in olive oil.

(I prefer peanut oil for frying.)

Drain on paper towels.

Boil the remainder of the eggplants in salted water or bake them in a moderate oven.

Cool.

Chop the onion and sauté in butter until pale gold.

Skin and chop the tomatoes.

Peel and mash the cooled boiled eggplants.

Mix together the mashed eggplant, the tomatoes, and the sautéed onion with 2 tablespoons of béchamel.

Season with salt, pepper and a pinch of cinnamon.

Butter a deep baking dish.

Alternate the sautéed eggplant slices and the eggplant mixture, sprinkling each layer with grated cheese.

4 pounds eggplant
Salt
Olive oil
2 large onions
Butter
3 ripe tomatoes
3 cups béchamel
Pepper
Cinnamon
½ pound grated Parmesan and
    Gruyère cheeses
3 eggs

Beat eggs into the béchamel and pour over the contents of the casserole.

Generously dust the surface with grated cheese.

Bake in a moderate oven approximately 30 minutes, until gold.

Serves six to eight.

## 130   Baked sea bass

*Spigola*, a variety of sea bass, is one of the luxury fishes of the Porto Ercole fish market.

We would bake it, first lining the tray of the oven with aluminum foil. We found the tray more convenient than a pan.

Slice the onions, tomatoes, and green peppers.

Pack some in the cavity of the bass with salt, pepper, and a nut of butter.

Close up the fish with toothpicks or small skewers.

Butter the aluminum foil at the bottom of the tray.

Place on it your sea bass.

Rub the skin with butter.

Season with salt, pepper, rosemary, and thyme.

Lay the slices of bacon over the top.

Arrange the remaining slices of onion, tomato, and green pepper around the fish.

Bake in a moderate oven for about 30 minutes, basting from time to time with the melted butter and white wine.

Serves four to five.

Our problem was that every one wanted second helpings.

The vegetables are a refreshing change from the usual bread crumb stuffings.

2 onions
2 tomatoes
2 green peppers
1 whole sea bass, 2 to 2½ pounds
Salt
Pepper
¼ pound butter
Rosemary
Thyme
4 slices bacon, blanched
½ cup white wine

## 131  Stuffed peppers Passetto

Everyone in Italy stuffs peppers. The restaurant Passetto in Rome gave me the recipe for their version. It couldn't be easier and everyone loves them.

Cut the top from the peppers.
Scoop out the seeds and the filaments.
In a bowl, mix the tuna fish, the pitted black olives, and the bread crumbs.
If the oil from the can of tuna fish is not enough to bind the stuffing, add a few drops of olive oil.
Stuff the peppers loosely with this mixture.
(I put back the caps.)
Set in a baking dish.
Dribble a bit of olive oil in the bottom and over the peppers.
Bake in moderate oven for 25 to 30 minutes.
The peppers will be a little underdone and deliciously *al dente*.
Serves four.

4 green peppers
1 pound canned tuna fish
18 black olives
Soft bread crumbs from 2 slices
    of bread
Oil

## 132  Miniature pizza

By reducing the size of the usual pizza down to a bite-size *pizzetta* or *pizzettina*, you can achieve a very elegant and amusing accompaniment to drinks. The dough is more reminiscent of a brioche.

Sift flour and salt together and cut in butter.
Add the yeast which has been dissolved in a little warm water, the egg, and milk.

*Pastry:*
2 cups sifted flour
½ tablespoon salt
2 tablespoons butter
1 teaspoon yeast
¼ cup warm water
1 egg
¼ cup milk

Work in well together and knead until smooth.
Repose the dough in a floured bowl.
Cover with a damp towel.
Let rest for 2 hours.
Roll dough thin.
Cut into small circles.
Place on greased baking sheets about 1½ inches apart.
Brush top of each pizza with a little olive oil.
The spreads can be varied, choosing assorted bits from the toppings mentioned at the right.
Sprinkle with oregano, chopped basil, or chopped parsley.
Moisten with a little olive oil.
Bake in a hot oven for 10 to 12 minutes.
Makes twenty-four to thirty miniature pizzas.

*Toppings:*
Mozzarella cheese
Anchovy
Mussels
Ham
Tomato
Artichoke hearts
Oregano
Basil
Grated Parmesan cheese
Parsley

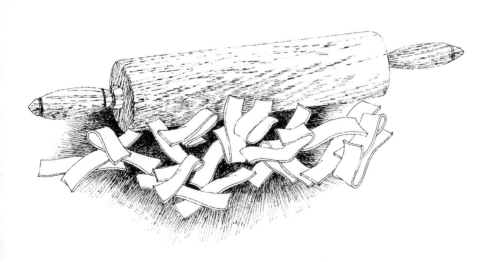

# Index